The Gang of Five

The Gang of Five

THE IMPACT OF FIVE GERMAN REFUGEE RABBINIC STUDENTS ON TWENTIETH-CENTURY REFORM JUDAISM

Richard Damashek

Cover photo: The Gang of Five at Hebrew Union College in Cincinnati, Ohio, 1935. Left to right: Leo Lichtenberg, Alfred Wolf, W. Gunther Plaut, Herman Schaalman, and Wolli Kaelter.

ISBN: 1540879097
ISBN 13: 9781540879097
Library of Congress Control Number: 2017900031
CreateSpace Independent Publishing Platform
North Charleston, South Carolina

Also by Richard Damashek

———

A Brand Plucked from the Fire: The Life of Rabbi Herman E. Schaalman (KTAV 2013); "Questioning God's Omnipotence and Omniscience: The Evidence in Torah," forthcoming in *The Life of Meaning: The Essential Guide to Reform Judaism*, edited by Dana Evans Kaplan (CCAR Press 2017); "The Gang of Five," forthcoming in *Reform Jewish Quarterly* (CCAR Press: fall 2017).

Reviews of previous work

———

"Herman E. Schaalman is one of the most distinguished Reform rabbis of twentieth-century America, someone who has lived the century with all its accomplishments and tragedies. In April 2015, he turned ninety-nine years old; he lives with his wife, Lotte, who recently turned one hundred. Richard Damashek, a retired English professor, now provides an appraisal of Schaalman's extraordinary life.

"A comprehensive account of Schaalman's life and philosophy was overdue; Damashek's book, *A Brand Plucked from the Fire: The Life of Rabbi Herman E. Schaalman*, has filled that void. The task was not easy since Schaalman has hardly published any of his thoughts, with the exception of *Hineni: Here I Am*, published when he was already more than ninety years old. Due to the lack of written sources, Damashek's biography heavily relies on interviews with Schaalman, his wife Lotte, as well as family members, friends, and colleagues. These interviews allow deep insight into the life and philosophy of Schaalman beyond the public rabbinic figure.

"Richard Damashek's biography of Herman E. Schaalman is a great work of research and writing on a remarkable personage, whose thinking is still progressing and who continues to live an active life, dedicated to his wife, his family, and the future of Judaism."

———

John T. Pawlikowski, OSM, PhD, professor and director, Catholic-Jewish Studies Program, Catholic Theological Union

"No one has done more over the years for positive Catholic-Jewish relations in Chicago than Herman Schaalman. He has provided an invaluable spiritual base for the dialogue but also served as an important, loving critic of both religious traditions. He has educated Christians and Jews alike and served as an instrument of reconciliation when necessary. Chicago would not be at the top of the interreligious dialogue world if God had not summoned him to minister in this city."

———

Rabbi Hillel Cohn, Rabbi Emeritus, Congregation Emanu El—San Bernardino/Redlands, rabbi, Sun City Jewish Congregation, San Bernardino, California

"Rabbi Herman Schaalman's life story deserves and needs to be told. He has served his congregations with extraordinary commitment, ministering to people of all ages and always leading them to take their Jewishness seriously. As a leader of the reform rabbinate, Rabbi Schaalman has led with the utmost of integrity and has always treated his colleagues with the utmost of respect. But most of all, he provides a model of what a thinking Jew ought to be: one who is never satisfied with what was, but always seeking new understandings. He doesn't ever stop thinking, re-assessing, questioning. This is evident throughout his life story but most of all in these later years of his life. What a blessing he is to the Jewish people and especially to his rabbinic colleagues who admire, respect, and love him."

————

Rabbi Barry Marks, Temple Israel, Springfield, Illinois

"It's a great story of a remarkable individual. Herman's friendship with Cardinal Bernardin is a very touching section of the book."

The Gang of Five: The Impact of Five German Refugee Rabbinic Students on Twentieth-Century Reform Judaism

Richard Damashek

Dedication

This book is dedicated to the Gang of Five
for their courage in coming to America,
a world they had not known,
to a seminary they had never heard of,
and who became a significant source of change
in twentieth-century Reform Judaism.
And to Rabbi Herman E. Schaalman,
my inspiration for writing this book
and for moving me along the path
to become a student of Torah.
Rabbi Schaalman died
at the age of one hundred,
only weeks before this book
was scheduled for publication
And to my wife, Jane Thomas,
who has waited patiently, with full support,
understanding, and love
while this five-year project was being completed.

Contents

Acknowledgments

———

First, I want to thank two Spertus Institute librarians, Kathy Bloch and Gail Goldberg, who found obscure documents in far-flung places. I'd also like to thank Kevin Proffitt and his staff at the American Jewish Archives for their diligence on my behalf.

Thanks, too, to the rabbis who graciously read the manuscript and provided commentary to address not only writing issues but also issues of content, particularly my judgments of the Gang's contributions to Reform Judaism. Special thanks to Rabbi Peter Knobel for his advice and endorsement of my efforts in bringing the lives of these remarkable rabbis to light, and Rabbi Michael Zedek.

Thank you to Dan Wolf for your willingness to read and proofread this text and to help set the record straight. From one writer to another, I can say your help has made this a better book, and thank you too for giving me access to your father's unpublished "Memories," without which a major portion of the book would be missing. And thanks for the proofreading assistance from Paul Thomann and Norman Karr, friends who are trudging along with me in our search for the meanings of Torah.

Thanks to the Tawani Foundation for its willingness to provide financial support for the publication of this book. Jennifer Pritzker has been most generous.

Foreword

————

THIS STORY IS INTERESTING AND extraordinary in its uniqueness. It is an attempt to put names and lives behind the fact that America was the recipient and savior of a whole set of assumptions in Judaism. None of the five of us had insignificant lives. Others have written that our lives had meaning for Reform Judaism. This book should be important for anyone interested in twentieth-century Reform Judaism. If anyone ignores us, they miss a major component of this development.

There were others, like Prinz and Baeck, who came over, and individually they made a much greater impression than any one of us, including Plaut. We came at a time when many asked what the whole question of what American Judaism would be like. We were the first stage of Jews coming from the old country to live here and shape lives and, if possible, make an impact on the land we thought of as primitive, a land of Indians and gangsters. Frankly, that's all we knew about America.

I don't think there was any other group like this that came to America during the Nazi period that was in any sense identifiable. And we remained in some fashion related all our lives. I'm the only one still alive, and I'm one hundred. Plaut was the eldest of us and died at the age of ninety-nine. I remember going to a meeting of rabbis in Toronto and calling him because he wasn't here. He said he was coming right over, but he was already disoriented. He had been a handsome, athletic man.

The story begins when five rabbinic students who were enrolled in Berlin's Liberal seminary, *Lehranstalt für die Wissenschaft des Judentums*, were selected to receive five scholarships offered by Hebrew Union College. Until the Nazis downgraded it, the Berlin seminary had been the *Hochschule für die Wissenschaft des Judentums*. I think it is remarkable that five students came over who had no affinity for each other. We were picked out of what must have been at least a hundred students.

Why were we selected? How come we were five? The main incentive for our selection was that there were five invitations, scholarships, that were sent from Hebrew Union College (HUC) in Cincinnati, Ohio. In the 1920s, HUC had sent over five faculty members to finish their studies there. So this was sort of a return engagement. There was no other reason why there were five of us chosen. We had no prior relationship with each other. We didn't know each other. I didn't even know their names until we met in Paris on the way to Le Havre to board a ship to America. We got to know each other on board the ship. So this is an indication of the fact that this union of refugee students was a total chance. There was no plan, no underlying reason why the five of us were picked.

We brought to this country a different kind of understanding of what it meant to be a rabbi in modern times. Speaking for myself, and I can include the others, we encountered a Judaism that to us was totally foreign and that challenged us to be who we were under those circumstances. None of us had been to America before. None of us spoke English in an acceptable fashion so that the acceptability of what we thought of America was primitive. It was also critical. We came as people who thought we knew more than anyone else. We came with a kind of anticipation that we were in a position and were meant to be teachers of people in America because they were primitive. We came with the assumption that we knew more, that we had an advantage over Americans, because we came from a culture that was more profound.

We changed HUC to the extent that we stuck together with each other and tried to change HUC culture, which we believed to be inferior to our own. We came with a certain prejudice. What we finally experienced was that the power of HUC religious life and culture was not only sufficient but actually superior to anything we had to offer. Within a year, I spoke English, and that changed so much. English is a powerful language. It is very expressive and has produced people of great caliber. We began to understand finally that this culture was a viable and vital culture, I mean Jewishly speaking. I am speaking for the five of us. Some of us came out more influenced, some less, by this culture. Kaelter, for example, whose father was a famous rabbi, wanted to retain more of the tradition from which he came.

We had a sense of attachment to our parents to a much stronger degree than the other students had to HUC. In our upbringing, our parents were the shapers of our understandings. But most important to know is that we didn't change HUC; HUC changed us. We came with the full expectation that we would bring culture to the institution and to American Reform Judaism. We would help to make it more traditional and therefore more Jewish. What we discovered was that Reform Judaism had so much more to offer us. It was richer than the Judaism we brought with us.

I think in retrospect that the '30s was one of the creative turning points in American Judaism. After that, there was not much. It was shaped into different images. Conservatism was a product of that period. You never need to shape Orthodoxy because they know who they are. They impose it. But the notion that there is a Judaism that has an

American stamp, that was something new, and in this development, we five had a major contribution to make and did.

The contribution we made to twentieth-century Reform Judaism was intensified practice. We were living our Judaism on a daily basis, and a few of us had come from intensely Jewish backgrounds. But in the long run, those of us who came from a less-intense Jewish background had a greater influence on us. In regard to mixed marriage and patrilineal descent, two of the major shaping forces in twentieth-century Reform Judaism, Plaut and I had enormous influence. Although we were unhappy with the proposed changes, we helped shape the final outcomes. We provided a brake on the enormity of the power behind the idea, the whole cultural shift behind the concept of mixed marriages. If its outcome had any kind of direction or shape, then Plaut and I played major roles in its development.

I'd like to say something too about the development of Reform Jewish camping. Both Wolf and Kaelter played important roles in its development on the West Coast. When I was the director of Olin Sang Ruby Union Institute in Oconomowoc, Wisconsin, I invited Kaelter to come and help me set it up. He not only served as one of the rabbinic faculty, but he provided a kind of youthful vigor that we needed to form bonds with the young campers. None of them had ever seen a rabbi slide into home base. It was in a swamp. I still remember yelling "Slide," and he did and then stood up covered in mud and dirt and who knows what else.

Perhaps the most important of us was Plaut. I admired him because he had traveled widely outside of Germany. He had been a top tennis player and had played in Palestine. He had opportunities to aspects of life that I never had. He came from a much more refined cultural life. Through his writings, his scholarship, his position within the rabbinate, he had a considerable impact on Reform Judaism. His was always a dominant one, even when he went to Canada. His commentary on the

Torah was a huge contribution. It was the first major commentary on the Hertz Torah in 1923.
  Rabbi Herman E. Schaalman
  August 23, 2016

Preface

————

THIS BOOK HAS ITS ORIGINS in my biography, *A Brand Plucked from the Fire: The Life of Rabbi Herman E. Schaalman.* The book is an in-depth study of Rabbi Schaalman's life and his contribution to American Reform Judaism. In it, I discuss briefly the other four German rabbinic students who came with him in 1935 on scholarship to Hebrew Union College in Cincinnati, Ohio: W. Gunther Plaut, Alfred Wolf, Wolli (Wolfgang) Kaelter, and Leo Lichtenberg. In my research, I discovered that no one had written a comprehensive article that traced their early lives in Germany, their rabbinic careers in the United States, their rise to national leadership in Reform Judaism, and their contributions to its development, not even Gunther Plaut, the most influential of them. The most extensive "articles" were their obituaries. I felt some guilt in propelling Rabbi Schaalman into the limelight while the rest of them remained unheralded. I was especially concerned that Plaut, who among them was the most prolific scholar and social justice advocate, had not received similar attention.

When they arrived in America, each was something of a pariah. Their fellow students didn't know what to make of them. Almost none of them spoke English, they wore "funny" clothes, and they stuck together as a kind of clique. One wag named them "the gang of five." It stuck, and from then on, the name became the tag for discussing the group of the precocious students.

In 1981, at the height of his powers, Plaut published *The Torah: A Modern Commentary*, the first such commentary in English since the publication of the Hertz *Pentateuch and Haftorahs* issued in the late 1920s and '30s. *The Torah: A Modern Commentary* received universal acclaim and established Plaut as the preeminent scholar of Reform Judaism. Reform congregations around the globe adopted the book, as did many Conservative congregations. Plaut's second major work, *Haftorah Commentary*, received universal critical acclaim and was adopted as a complement to *The Torah: A Modern Commentary*. Together, these two books were the capstone to Plaut's remarkable and brilliant career. As the prodigious and successful scholar and rabbi that he was, he deserves a biography of his own.

Rabbis Wolf's and Kaelter's most important contributions to twentieth-century Reform came in their work to establish Reform Jewish camping on the West Coast, particularly in California. In that, they extended the work of Rabbi Schaalman, who shepherded the creation of the first Reform camp in Oconomowoc, Wisconsin. Their contributions are discussed in Gary Zola and Michael Lorge, *A Place of Their Own: The Rise of Reform Jewish Camping* (2006).

Unfortunately, there are precious few documents available for Rabbi Lichtenberg. I could not find published assessments of his career as a rabbi. Only two original source documents exist: one by his daughter Ruth Levor, a transcript of a speech she gave about her father at an HUC-JIR commemoration ceremony; and the other by his wife, Hilda, an interview she gave about herself and her husband.

Much of the material about Plaut and Kaelter comes from their autobiographies; the information about Schaalman from the more than one hundred hours of interviews I conducted with him and recorded in his biography; and most of the information about Wolf comes from an unpublished three-hundred-page work entitled *Collected Memories,* which his son, Dan Wolf, kindly allowed me to read.

The Gang of Five is intended to bring to light significant parts of the lives of these distinguished rabbis and assess their contributions to Reform Judaism, which, in my view, is long overdue.

Introduction

———

IN LATE AUGUST 1935, FIVE young German rabbinic students left their homeland and set out for America on an adventure that would transform their lives and help shape twentieth-century Reform Judaism. The students—Herman Schaalman, W. Gunther Plaut, Alfred Wolf, Wolli Kaelter, and Leo Lichtenberg—had been selected by their seminary president to receive scholarships that had been offered by Hebrew Union College, Reform Judaism's seminary in Cincinnati, Ohio.[1] They left Berlin's renowned Liberal *Lehranstalt Für die Wissenschaft des Judentums* for the uncertainty of a journey to America's heartland, a place they knew nothing about, for study at an institution they had never heard of, bound for experiences they had never dreamed of.[2] Unknown to them at the time, their departure was an appointment with destiny.

Why did they go? Faced with an increasingly difficult situation for German Jews, not only were their seminary administrators and faculty concerned for their futures in Germany, but so too were their parents. Who were these young men? How did they see themselves? What impact did they have on twentieth-century Reform Judaism? Each of them had a separate story to tell. Thanks to the publication of Schaalman's biography, Plaut's and Kaelter's autobiographies, and Wolf's extensive, but unpublished memoirs, we know a great deal about them but very little about Lichtenberg.[3] Considering them in order of their contributions to Reform Judaism, Plaut comes first, followed by Schaalman, Wolf, Kaelter, and finally Lichtenberg.

PART 1

Two Seminaries Collaborate in Response to Nazi Threat

——————

IN 1935, HEBREW UNION COLLEGE (HUC), the citadel of Reform Judaism in America, offered its Berlin counterpart, *Lehranstalt für die Wissenschaft des Judentums*, five scholarships for its rabbinic students to attend the Cincinnati-based seminary.[4] The story behind this offer begins in the 1920s when HUC sent five of its faculty to study at the Liberal Berlin seminary.[5] Although worlds apart geographically, the two seminaries had much in common. HUC had been founded by *Lehranstalt* graduates, and members of the HUC Board of Governors had parents or grandparents who were German immigrants.[6] Moreover, HUC's American-born faculty members, including the college president, Dr. Julian Morgenstern, had received their doctorates at Berlin universities and had intimate acquaintances among German Jews. Very likely, there was also a humanitarian motive. In 1935, HUC was aware of the increasing dangers for Jews in Germany and that the very survival of German Jewry was in jeopardy. The HUC Board of Governors decided to reciprocate the *Lehranstalt*'s hosting of five HUC faculty with its offer of five scholarships.[7]

Part of the agreement between the two seminaries was that if conditions permitted, the students would return to Germany once they were ordained. If that were not possible or desirable, they would remain in the United States, where they would seek rabbinic positions. To HUC's credit, despite its own financial difficulties and the lack of pulpit vacancies for its own students, the college decided to underwrite the students' expenses.[8]

By June 1935, the president of the Berlin seminary, Ismar Elbogen, and faculty member Leo Baeck had selected two of the five students, Wolli Kaelter and Gunther Plaut.[9] Kaelter was part of a group of students whom the president and his wife hosted regularly. At one of these events, Elbogen asked, "Herr Kaelter, how would you like to continue your studies in America? Dr. Baeck and I thought that you and Plaut would most likely be very much interested, and that it would be good to send you."[10] Although Kaelter did not take the offer seriously at first, he told Elbogen he had to consult his mother. She objected, but when he told her that he would take advantage of all the cultural opportunities and that he would return in a year, she let him go. That was all the assurance his parents needed.

Plaut may have been selected first. On April 27, 1935, the day after Passover, Professor Leo Baeck called him into his office and offered him the opportunity to continue his rabbinic studies at Hebrew Union College in America. He told Plaut it was "a splendid place." Plaut didn't hesitate: "I knew at once I wanted to go."[11] To get approval from his parents, he had to promise he would return in two years. Plaut's father wasn't taking any chances and bought him a round-trip ticket.[12]

Kaelter thought the decision to send him and Plaut "was rather random."[13] When the seminary announced that three more scholarships were available, five other students applied. Subsequently, one of them dropped out because his family wouldn't let him go. Now there were four finalists for the remaining three slots: Herman Schaalman, Alfred Wolf, Leo Lichtenberg, and Heinz Schneemann.

In Wolf's account, the invitation to attend HUC "came like the answer to a prayer." Conditions for Jews in Germany were rapidly deteriorating. A few days before he knew about the scholarship possibility, Wolf wrote in his "Collected Memories," "My parents and I had a conversation about the desirability of my leaving Germany. Apart from relatives in the Netherlands, we had no 'foreign' contacts, and the relatives living outside Germany were 'too close for comfort' near the German border."[14] When he informed Elbogen that he was applying for one of the scholarships, Elbogen requested an approval from his parents. They were only too happy to give it, and Alfred became one of the finalists. Nonetheless, like Plaut's parents, they bought him a round-trip ticket so he could come home after two years during his summer break. Getting out of Nazi Germany was a huge relief for Alfred: "I remember that I literally breathed more easily the moment my train crossed the border into France."

At the end of June, Elbogen brought the four applicants together in a room adjoining his office and told them that they had fifteen minutes to decide which three of them would go. When they had made their decision, they were to knock on the door to his study, enter and close the door.

For the young Herman Schaalman, who did not want to go but had been pushed by his father to enter the competition, suddenly everything changed: "All of a sudden, destiny was knocking on the door... Each student tried to figure out reasons why the others should not go."[15] After several rounds of votes, Schneemann, whom both Schaalman and Kaelter reported did not want to leave his fiancée, announced that he was not going and left the room. The three remaining finalists knocked on Elbogen's door. When the door opened, they told him they would accept the scholarships. Elbogen replied, "Congratulations. You are going to America."[16]

The five finalists knew next to nothing about America. For Schaalman, it was not only a strange land, but "uncivilized Indian territory...the wild west...gangster territory..." Had he been asked to name all the German emperors, their mistresses, and the German kings, he could rattle them off. But he had never heard of Cincinnati, or for that matter, Hebrew Union College. He didn't even know Cincinnati was a city until he looked it up in his encyclopedia. According to Plaut, although the students knew little about HUC, they assumed that their education at the Berlin seminary would be more than adequate to meet all requirements and that HUC would be religiously comparable to the Berlin institution. In both respects, they found out otherwise.

Leaving home was not easy for Schaalman or Wolf.[17] For Schaalman, it was heartbreaking: "I will never forget hanging out of the window of the train of the Munich station and waving a handkerchief and seeing my family's handkerchiefs waving goodbye. And somehow or other, I had an anticipation...I felt terribly lost and alone."[18] At the time, he had no idea that he would see his parents and brothers only once in the next twelve years.

Wolf remembered a deep sense of loss:

I was leaving all I had known for something that was yet unknown but showed great promise for my future. So, there was a great deal of uncertainty and a certain amount of worry mixed in with my high expectations for 'the new place'...I was leaving a place that had ceased to be the only home I ever knew and which, outside of the walls of the paternal and grandpaternal homes, no longer felt like home at all.[19]

Faced with an increasingly difficult situation for German Jews, not only were the *Lehranstalt* administrators and faculty worried about their futures in Germany, but so too were the young men's parents. Germany was moving quickly toward becoming a police state. Anti-Semitism had become state policy and violence against Jews was becoming part of daily life. From the beginning of the Nazi ascendancy, Jews became the object of ever-increasing and menacing legislation aimed at demonizing them and depriving them of their civil rights, their livelihoods, and their property. Despite the violence and the economic discrimination, in 1935 German Jews did not know that the Nazis would soon turn their full savagery on them in an attempt to exterminate all of them.

PART 2

Early Life in Germany

———

W. GUNTHER PLAUT

> *"I have often wondered what course my life would have taken had I accepted [the scholarship to attend Stanford in 1932] and found myself in the United States at the time when Hitler came to power. I might never have returned; I might instead have finished law school in California. And I would certainly never have entered the rabbinate."*[20]

WORDS WELL WORTH PONDERING FROM a rabbi who made such an indelible contribution to Judaism. An even more profound question is: what would Reform Judaism have been without his contribution?

Gunther Plaut was the eldest of the Gang of Five and had gone further in his rabbinic training than the others. When Schaalman met him in the *Lehranstalt*, Plaut already had a doctorate in law and had achieved recognition as a tennis pro. He had represented Germany in the Maccabee Games in Palestine as a professional tennis player and saw himself as "a man of the world with great self-confidence, a leader type."

Born in Münster, Germany, on November 1, 1912, Gunther was the older of the two sons of Jonas and Selma Plaut. Not long after he was born, his family moved to Berlin, where his father was hired to run a

Jewish orphanage. Gunther and his brother, Walter, grew up with the orphans as their playmates.

Just prior to the beginning of World War I, Gunther noticed that people began wearing uniforms as a sign of their patriotism. One day, his father came home wearing a uniform embellished with a sidearm. Because of his poor eyesight, Jonas was assigned to the War Ministry, where he mostly compiled death lists.

According to Plaut, the war years "changed the face of my neighborhood." The streets were mostly empty of men, and because leather was needed for the soldiers' boots, shoes were scarce. Even food became a problem; by 1917, the Allied blockade had effectively cut off food supplies. Because Gunther's father worked in the War Ministry, the Plauts were trapped in Berlin. Mostly, they ate potatoes and herring. Occasionally, despite the dangers of being accused of hoarding food, Selma would venture out of the city to buy meat from nearby farmers, who were never without food. She also had her own garden in which she grew vegetables.

World War I took a heavy toll on the Plaut family. Gunther's uncles, Max and Walter, were killed in the battle of Verdun: "For the first time, I began to understand what sorrow meant."[21] His was not the only family to suffer such losses; more than two million German soldiers died in the war.

As Germany teetered on the brink of defeat and revolution, its social fabric was being torn apart. For Gunther, who was only six years old when the war ended in 1918, the explosive energy of a repressed society was palpable and infectious, and men both in and out of uniform carried guns in the street. Left- and right-wing forces were fighting a ferocious battle for dominance. And then, without any particular fanfare, the Austrian government released Adolf Hitler from prison, an act that gave rise to the National Socialist Party.

Life in Germany was so disrupted that Gunther's parents decided to keep him out of the public schools and homeschooled him until he was eight. Although at first he was behind the other students in public school, he soon caught up and excelled, becoming number two in his public-school class.

In 1922, Gunther's father took over the directorship of the Auerbach orphanage. Founded in the nineteenth century as a Jewish institution, it was well respected in the community. Because it was located at the northern end of Berlin, Gunther had to change schools, but he quickly became the top student in his grade.

Part of the regimen of the school required the director's family to live on the grounds, but even more importantly for Gunther's development, the orphanage's daily routine meant that the children were immersed in Judaism, including a requirement that they participate in daily prayers. Moreover, a Liberal Jewish congregation, cofounded by his father, met in a 250-seat synagogue above the Plaut apartment.

Gunther was deeply affected by this new closeness to Judaism. Thereafter, he noted, his life as a Jew became part of his everyday experience: "Everyone I knew attended Jewish classes in public school, and everyone I knew was a bar mitzvah."[22] On Shabbat, he attended Friday night services with his father in the synagogue above their apartment: "It would never have occurred to me to say I had something else to do or that I did not feel like going. Attending Friday night services, and later, when I had finished high school, Saturday mornings, was a normal as breathing."[23]

Although Gunther was an outstanding student, these years were challenging for him in another way. Compared to his schoolmates, he was small and unable to compete with them. He was also woefully ignorant about sex. When they talked about girls and boasted of their sexual experiences, he could only listen and feel even smaller than he was. He was so naive that he didn't know the physiological difference between the sexes.

By the time he was fourteen, his competitive spirit kicked in, and he promised himself that he would be top in athletics as well as in academics. His first choice was track and field, and later tennis. He trained himself for track and field by running 1,500 meters around that orphanage courtyard. In the next school meet, he won first place, a surprise to everyone—including himself.

Gunther took up tennis as his next athletic passion. He read everything he could find about how to play the game. Again, he used the meager facilities at his disposal to develop and then hone his skills. The orphanage courtyard again became his training ground where he practiced hitting balls against a wall. After seeing the famous tennis champ Bill Tilden play an exhibition game, he was more determined than ever to become an expert player. The first time he played on a real court, he was in a high school tournament. Remarkably, he took second place. As a result, he gained the respect of the boys who had been taunting him, and this ended their abuse.

Life as a young boy had compensations. As early as the age of eight, he joined a Zionist youth group. The Plauts were not Zionists and did not encourage their son's joining. Zionism had no appeal to Plaut's father, who believed he had a hereditary right to remain in Germany. After all, he could trace his German family roots back hundreds of years. What he didn't see was that Germany was soon to become hostile to his very life.

The emergence of Zionism as an interest of Jewish youth may be explained in part as a response to the growing anti-Semitism that placed severe limitations on their ability to find a meaningful place in German society. Recognizing the value of such organizations, the German Jewish community formed its own groups, including sports clubs and various youth movements. At first, most Jewish youth chose apolitical activities, and some turned to escapist diversions such as social activities and cheap amusements. They were also attracted by the increasingly permissive sexual mores in the big cities.

The Zionist group that Plaut joined was the counterpart of the other German youth groups that excluded Jews. For Gunther, the Zionist group provided the opportunity for "endless discussions" and lots of hiking. Hiking meant living outdoors, staying in youth hostels, sitting around campfires, and endless debates about everything, including what it meant to be Jewish and the relationship of Jews to Germans.

Life in Germany in the 1920s was moving quickly in the direction of a Nazi takeover. In 1922, the symbol of democratic socialism, Walter Rathenau, Germany's foreign minister and a Jew, was assassinated. The ten-year-old Plaut recognized that this development was serious but was too young to understand its full significance. His father did and told his son, "Remember this day. It bodes ill for Germany and worse for the Jews."[24]

Plaut described this event "as a watershed" in his life. He was aware that he was a Jew and that this fact carried special significance, but the fact that his father was so deeply troubled altered his life: "For me, my childhood was over. I was growing up."[25] Nevertheless, because of the protected environment of the orphanage, he could avoid the confrontation with the alarming growth of anti-Semitism promoted by the Nazis. This is not to say that he was not affected by the social turmoil going on around him:

I spent eight long years in an environment of increasing unrest and violence. Inflation was beginning to ravage the country to a degree unparalleled in history. The postage stamp which yesterday had cost a few pfennigs would cost a hundred marks shortly after, and then the price went to a thousand, a million, and more.[26]

When he enrolled in the public high school, he came face-to-face with the growing anti-Semitism. After Hitler was released from prison in 1924 and *Mein Kampf* was published in 1925, anti-Semitism became more pronounced in the schools and soon threatened Gunther's well-being. Every day, the boy sitting in front of him would take advantage of the teacher's absence from the room to turn around and hit him "squarely in the mouth," and declare, "You shitty Jew, that's yours for the day."[27] At first Gunther suffered these attacks because he was much smaller than his tormentor, but after a while he became so accustomed to his assault that "even the dread...faded away."

Attacks like this were not unusual for Jewish schoolchildren, who were often the butt of anti-Semitic abuse. As Germany drifted toward Nazism, they had to cope not only with abuse from other students, but increasingly from their teachers. This daily bullying and harassment by both students and teachers made school life more difficult in the classroom and on the school grounds. To further humiliate their Jewish students, schools now set aside "isolation desks for Jews," and school authorities modified the curriculum to include daily discussions of the "Jewish Question." While their classmates stared at them as members of a despised race, Jewish children had to sit through these discussions, no matter how demeaning and humiliating. To make matters worse, they were often called to the front of the class to demonstrate the 'typical Jewish racial features.'

Plaut's sense of physical inferiority took a sharp turn when he floored another boy who had finally tormented him beyond his threshold for taking abuse. The fact that Gunther could flatten this boy, whom he thought of as much bigger than himself, came as a surprise. He then discovered that he had grown as tall as the others, was a better athlete than most of them, and was in better shape. To give himself an added advantage, he took lessons in jujitsu and was never bothered again. He learned from this experience was that "anti-Semites thrive on Jewish weakness and fear" and that their aggressive posture "evaporates in the face of strength and guts."

Even though he lived in a Jewish milieu at the orphanage, Plaut described his Jewish upbringing as "more cultural than religious." The daily religious activities that were part of his life at the orphanage, his attendance at holiday services, and the practice of Judaism in his home were all part of his environment. He did not understand the experience as religious, nor did it direct him to become a rabbi. Such a calling had never crossed his mind.

Despite his challenges in high school, Gunther managed to engage in what we would call extracurricular activities. In one of them, he became a member of the Society for French-German Understanding. Most of its members were adults, but he and his friend, Bruno Sommerfeld, joined to learn French for the intellectual excitement it offered. As a member, he had his first introduction to Freud, particularly *Totem and Taboo*, though the book proved to be "too advanced for him."

On the other hand, as a member of the society, he had the opportunity to be part of an exchange program with France, and he grabbed it. A whole new world opened for him, intellectually, culturally, and socially. His housing was near an area where prostitutes roamed the streets:

> One evening, as I stood looking at a shop window, a young woman hardly older than I stood next to me. Before I knew what was happening, she had taken my hand, exposed her breast, and made me touch it.
> "You like it?" she invited me.
> I fled in terror.[28]

At this point in his life, he was in high school and still knew nothing about girls or sex. He had no female friends, had never been on a date, and had never been at a party where girls were present.

Growing up in Germany during the 1920s was not without its pleasures and excitements. Despite the growing anti-Semitism, Berlin took part in the Roaring Twenties. Plaut described the city as a "fantastic place in which to grow up." Although he was too young to participate in many of its activities, the city was alive with some of the greatest artists and art venues of the twentieth century. It was the home of conductors such as Leo Blech, Otto Klemperer, Wilhelm Furtwängler, and Bruno Walter; and literary and theater greats such as Max Reinhardt, Ernest Toller, Rainer Maria Rilke, Thomas Mann, Jacob Wassermann, Arnold Zweig, and Franz Werfel. The city was no less alive with scientific geniuses such as Einstein and Planck, who were reinventing twentieth-century physics. "Berlin," wrote Plaut, "was a great city, and its ambiance rubbed off on the young man who was now ready to enter university."[29]

Unlike other members of the Gang of Five, who knew at a young age that they wanted to be rabbis, Plaut wanted to study law. From his father, he picked up the suggestion that he might take over the orphanage when Jonas retired. In the meantime, Jonas suggested that Gunther should study law, which would give him many new career opportunities, including civil servant, diplomat, judge and lawyer. Gunther's cousin Leo offered to take him into his firm.

When Gunther entered law school at the University of Berlin in 1930, he had no idea what was in store for him. Not only was it a gateway for him to study law, it opened a whole new world of association with women. For the first time in his life, he found himself in a co-ed environment. Although now in the university, he still had had no contact with women, which meant that he didn't even know how to talk to women, especially to attractive women who were all around him.

Gunther decided to make a foray into politics and joined the Social Democratic Students' Union. He didn't stay long, because he didn't like the way it was run. At the university, because attendance was optional, he didn't attend many classes. One class he did attend was Martin Wolf's class on contracts and civil law. Wolf lectured in a large auditorium filled with students. He was so popular that many of the students were not even registered. Even though Wolf was a Jew, students wearing swastikas on their lapels came to hear him.

During these heady days, Gunther took up soccer, but not at the university. His team was made up of local working-class men, and he was the only Jew on the team. Nevertheless, even though anti-Semitism was rampant throughout German society, in the three years he played in this league, he never experienced an anti-Semitic slander.

At one point, his parents thought it would be good for their son to have experience living independently, so his mother sent him for a semester to the University of Heidelberg. There, he joined the university's varsity soccer team and participated in competitions in southern Germany and France. So thoroughly did he throw himself into this sport that he neglected his studies and failed one of his courses. After that humiliation, he vowed never to let that happen again.

But he couldn't give up his love of sports. He must have been a restless young man who needed an outlet for his prodigious energies. Not only was he passionately engaged in soccer and chess, but he also took up his earlier love of tennis. Again, he found that he was falling behind in his studies.

Heidelberg was not a peaceful town. The Nazis organized political disturbances that frequently turned violent. Gunther, unable to ignore what was going on, again joined the Social Democratic Students' Union. The members, however, tended to be peaceful idealists who were no match for the much more passionate Communists and Nazis.

One of Gunther's assignments for the Union was to distribute propaganda flyers on a street corner. On one occasion, he found himself surrounded by a gang of six Nazis who were part of a fencing fraternity.

They knocked the flyers out of his hand and were about to pounce on him. But they were in for a rude shock. By this point in Gunther's life, he was confident enough in his own physical abilities that he decided to fight back. When he turned on them, they backed off, stunned that he would resist them. One of the young men spat on the ground, and then they walked away. Gunther felt empowered. In his mind, the experience had made him a man.

This was only the beginning of his confrontation with Nazis. When he returned to Berlin, the Nazis had become more aggressive. Street brawls were so common that Gunther could not avoid them.

However, in 1932 he had a chance to get out of Germany. Stanford University offered him a scholarship, but a dean at his university in Berlin advised him not to take it. He told Gunther that whatever he learned about law in the United States would be of no use in Germany, where the law was very different. In *Unfinished Business*, Plaut raised the issue of his inability to see the handwriting on the wall. He concluded that German Jews had lived so long in the chaos and vicious anti-Semitism following WWI, that these conditions had become normal.

Nonetheless, he felt a dual allegiance, one as a German citizen and the other as a Jew. He tried to live in two worlds at once: at home, he was a Jew, and on the streets, he was a German. The streets were becoming scary, and he could feel the encroaching insanity, but when he was at home, all was peaceful, and his fears disappeared.

He finished law school on January 30, 1933, just as Hitler came to power. The streets immediately erupted with the raucous sound of storm troopers carrying torches through the darkened streets. They were singing, "When Jewish blood spurts from our knives, things will go twice as well."[30] This new development was enough to finally clinch for Gunther his mistake in not accepting the scholarship to Stanford. In his autobiography, he made this astonishing admission:

I have often wondered what course my life would have taken
had I accepted and found myself in the United States at the
time when Hitler came to power. I might never have returned;
I might instead have finished law school in California. *And I
would certainly never have entered the rabbinate* [italics added].[31]

Instead, "the gradualness of much of the Nazis' official anti-Semitic
program" dulled his senses to the threats he was facing. Other German
Jews, who also experienced this false sense of security, turned inward to
live what Plaut described as "an exclusively Jewish ambiance: in theater,
in music, and in sports."

Gunther and his family accepted second-class citizenship relatively
easily. They realized that from the beginning they had never been full
citizens, and the slow erosion of their rights made the awareness of the
loss a matter of degree.

Plaut found a partial escape from this paralyzing reality by joining two Jewish sports organizations: Kahoah to play soccer, and Bar
Kochba to play tennis again. With Kahoah, Gunther traveled to various
cities to play against other Jewish soccer teams. When he played tennis
against other Jewish teams, the experience was no different than when
he was playing against Germans. The excitement was there, as well as
the desire to win, and he did—he won the German-Jewish champion-
ship in tennis singles. For Gunther, this period provided a psychological
escape from the reality of living as a Jew in Nazi Germany.

As a student during these turbulent times, Gunther had to give up
his gentile friends and withdraw from many of the extracurricular activities he loved. He took refuge in the university library to study for his
exams. In 1934, at the age of twenty-two, Gunther emerged from his
self-imposed cocoon to take his law exams. Although he passed hand-
ily, the Nazis had decreed that no Jews would be allowed to intern, a

precondition for admission to the Bar. The fact that the Nazis had put an end to his dream of practicing law changed his life forever.

Now he had to look at other options for a career. He thought of continuing his legal studies in Britain, but he realized that because British law was utterly different, he'd have to start all over again. The family proposed other possibilities, including getting a doctorate in law from another German university. Gunther went to Heidelberg to investigate this option. He sought help from Professor Lewy but was rejected because he had failed one of Lewy's courses. His next stop was Erlangen, a university that was well known to have loose standards but was "summarily refused" because he was not Aryan.

Upon Gunther's return to Berlin, he paid a visit to his former professor, Hans Lewald, who was half Jewish. To Gunther's surprise, Lewald accepted him as a doctoral student, and Professor Wolf agreed to cosponsor him. Not long after Gunther began his course of studies, he got approval for his thesis topic, "The Nullity of Marriage in German and Swiss International Law." Six months later, when he presented his thesis, Lewald accepted it, but Wolf rejected it and Gunther was "crushed."

He could not easily approach the professor for a meeting to discuss his rejection. During this period, students did not dare to argue with a professor, especially one who was considered the best legal mind in Germany. Out of desperation, Gunther did it anyway, but the professor wasn't buying Gunther's arguments: "Herr Plautt [*sic*], I don't buy a single word of what you say, and I stand by my previous judgment [*sic*]. Your argument is worthless. But your persistence and nerve are admirable. I will close both my eyes and let your thesis pass."[32] With that, Gunther went on to pass his written and oral exams and became Herr Doctor Gunther Plaut. He now had a doctorate and a law degree. Nonetheless, he still couldn't work as either a lawyer or a professor in Germany.

His father, still certain that the Nazi regime would be short-lived, advised his son to try something else that was still open to Jews. He proposed that Gunther enroll in the *Lehranstalt für die Wissenschaft des Judentums*, Berlin's Liberal Jewish seminary. Gunther demurred. He didn't think he knew enough Hebrew to handle the studies. Though he could read Hebrew in the prayer book, he didn't know any more Hebrew than that. Anticipating Gunther's objection, Jonas had already hired a tutor so that during the summer, his son could prepare for entry in the fall. Gunther accepted the proposal and thought learning more Hebrew would be a good idea. He had always been good at languages. Like so many other Jews during this period, he felt a need to identify more closely with being Jewish. Many years later, he explained, if he were made to suffer for it, he wanted to know what it meant to be truly Jewish. The seminary was another way to shut out the bitter realities of his shrinking universe, and retreat into a domain that had not been touched by the Nazis.

Little did Gunther know at the time that the tutor was Abraham Joshua Heschel, who would become one of the great philosophers of the twentieth century. When the two encountered each other, Heschel was only a few years older than Gunther. Under Heschel's tutelage, Gunther quickly discovered that he knew even less than he thought. When he began taking courses in the fall of 1934 at the *Lehranstalt*, he found that he still didn't know enough. His lessons were painstaking: what others could do in an hour took him all day. He was persistent, however, and gradually caught on.

Although he had no intention of becoming a rabbi, he took a course in homiletics (the art of preaching) from the famous Jewish scholar Leo Baeck. Aware of Baeck's fame, Gunther felt privileged to sit in his class. He also studied history and Talmud with the famous Talmudic scholar Ismar Elbogen. The seminary helped change Gunther's life. Prior to enrollment, he never thought twice about riding on Shabbat, but now he had to quit to follow the seminary's rules. That meant when he and fellow students wanted to visit Professor Elbogen on Shabbat after services, they had to walk forty-five minutes to get to his house.

Part of Gunther's training was to give occasional sermons as a student preacher, first at youth services and later at adult services outside of Berlin. In his first outings, he stuck to biblical texts as his source. However, as the Nazis tightened their hold on Germany, he turned his sermons into political attacks by using biblical references to mask his criticism. His text was Jacob and Edom. In Jewish tradition, Edom was equated with oppressors throughout the ages. Gunther included part of that sermon in his autobiography:

> It is easier to rule men by force than to rule their hearts. It is easier to succeed by violence than by the spirit...Each generation stands anew against Edom to assert its right...We must never cease to struggle, never cease to hope...Those who bless you, I will bless, and curse him who curses you.[33]

The effect of the Nazi threat was that Jews flocked to their synagogues. Attendance swelled, and Plaut noted that even he, "the unlearned young student," drew a respectable crowd. Most important for him now was the growing recognition that he was making a serious commitment to a life he had never dreamed of. He was now developing a missionary spirit directed to the survival of Judaism.

Even his tennis activities played an important role in his religious development. His tennis friends brought him in contact with the Jewish upper crust, where he met young men and women who routinely traveled abroad, owned cars, and for whom money wasn't an issue. These were the Jews whose "Judaism had evaporated," that is, until the Nazis reminded them that they could not escape being Jews. Now that he had access to this high social stratum, he found himself functioning as a sort of guru for young Jewish men and women from wealthy homes. He was a well-known athlete, an intellectual with a penchant for philosophizing, a "student of Judaica, and a Zionist." These characteristics proved to be a magnet for the uninitiated Jews. He found his sudden popularity dazzling and a hot item for young, attractive girls.

His parents worried that this new social involvement might not be good for him. They hadn't had any experience with wealthy Jews and were fearful that the values of money and materialism might turn their son away from the values they had instilled. "Be careful," his father admonished, "you're not in their league."[34] For Gunther, the warning was superfluous. The time had come when all Jews were in the same league.

He also realized that he had not been able to make male friends. His cousin Leo had warned him about his arrogance, but because of his success in athletics and academics, he had developed "what must be called an insufferable edge of arrogance." He was, however, more successful with women. Nevertheless, he realized that his self-image was based on insecurity as well as conceit. Later, he wrote in his autobiography that his earlier behavior was socially and emotionally immature.

In 1935, Gunther traveled to Palestine to participate in the second Jewish Olympic Games. He went with some two hundred Jewish athletes from the German Maccabi, the Jewish sports federation, and his mother, who went along to see relatives in Palestine. Gunther was ranked second on the tennis team and was a member of the soccer team as well. For the first leg of the journey, they traveled by ship to Haifa and then boarded a train to Tel Aviv. On the ship, Gunther met Martin Buber was also traveling to Palestine. His meeting Buber left a lifelong impression on Gunther.

Jewish athletes from all over the world came to the games. Although at one point, Gunther's group considered remaining in Palestine, the strict immigration quota for Jews made that impossible. They were also bound by their promises to return to Germany. To his surprise, Gunther realized that despite his commitment to Zionism, it was mostly an intellectual commitment, not one he was willing to act upon.

The games proved to be a disappointment. The courts weren't up to his usual standards, the sunlight in Tel Aviv was too strong, and the heat oppressive. When the games ended, Gunther and his mother traveled around the country, and what he saw amazed him. The people were so unlike the Jews he had known. They were idealistic, optimistic, and wonderfully effective in transforming the inhospitable desert in which they lived. He visited kibbutzim and fell in love with the people and the spirit that animated them. Most of all, he observed that the people were free, and that their lives provided a stark contrast to the Jewish life in Germany. In later years, he could not help but wonder what his life might have been like had he stayed.

HERMAN SCHAALMAN

*Get yourself ready! Stand up and say to
them whatever I command you.
Do not be terrified by them, or I will terrify you before them.
Today I have made you a fortified city, an
iron pillar, and a bronze wall
to stand against the whole land against the kings of Judah,
its officials, its priests, and the people of the land.
They will fight against you but will not overcome you,
for I am with you and will rescue you, declares the LORD.*
Julian Morgenstern, 1941

With these words, Dr. Julian Morgenstern, president of Hebrew Union College, sent off the newly minted Rabbi Herman E. Schaalman into the world of twentieth-century Reform Judaism. As part of the ordination ceremony for each graduating class, Morgenstern invited each ordinee to stand with him in front of the ark of the seminary's synagogue. Then, he would whisper in the ordinee's ear words of encouragement and blessing that reflected his sense of the student's destiny. When he heard these words on May 26, 1941, Schaalman had no expectation that one day he would have a significant impact on Reform Judaism. Schaalman was fond of saying, "Things happened to me that I could never have predicted nor expected."[35]

Born in Munich on April 28, 1916, to Adolf and Regina (nee Wanschel) Schaalman, Herman was the first son of a family of three brothers, including Ernst and Manfred, the youngest. His parents decided to marry just before Adolf was drafted and sent to the front. Nine months after he came home on leave, Regina gave birth to their first son. Adolf had come home on furlough to be present at the birth, but the birth was late. He decided to return to his company, so as not to waste the few additional days of his furlough. When news arrived that his son had been born, Adolf was granted leave to go home for the *bris*. On his way to the train station, a messenger overtook him and reported that the shelter in which he had been living for the last two years had taken a direct hit, killing everyone in it. From that time forward, Adolf credited his son's birth for saving his life.

Because of the Allies' naval blockade, food in Germany was scarce. Regina knew that food was more plentiful in the mountains, so she took her son to an Alpine village. In exchange for milk and bread from local farmers, she took a job as an organist in a nearby church. When the war ended in 1918, she returned to Munich. Until then, Herman had never met his father. When the two-year-old heard a noise in the foyer of his home, he went to see what was happening. A strange man dressed in a uniform was taking off his belt and fatigue cap and hanging them in the wardrobe. Herman began to scream. For the next several days, father and son worked at getting to know each other.

The Schaalmans were part of the intellectual upper crust of the city, where education and position mattered. The fact that Adolf was a professor gave the family prestige and respect. An important part of Herman's growing up was the level of education and cultural sophistication in his home. His father was a university graduate, a scientist, and a scholar of Judaism and Jewish history. Regina was also an intellectual and avid reader. She loved poetry and music. When she was alone, she sang and played her favorite Mozart arias on the family piano. For Herman, "These were special, though rare, moments...I used to sneak in, squat down next to the piano, and put my ear to it to hear the music transmitted through its innards."[36]

Adolf also contributed to the musical environment that was part of the Schaalman home. On special occasions, he sang arias and Handel oratorios while accompanied on the piano by a colleague. He was such a great Wagnerian aficionado that it was not unusual to hear him sing passages at home. Because he was also fond of Jewish liturgical music, hardly a day passed when he wasn't chanting the daily prayer service to his son. This early saturation in music helped Herman develop his own interest in singing. At one point, it gave him reason to think he might become a cantor.

At a time when women were not normally enrolled in higher education, Regina attended a nearby university to get a degree in chemistry and biology. That is, until she had to quit because taking care of Herman and attending the university turned out to be too difficult. Because the family couldn't afford a babysitter, she brought Herman with her, though he was only two-and-a-half when she started. Having him with her turned out to be a formidable obstacle. As one of the few women in the university, she also ran into the male-only confederacy. Some of her professors refused to teach the class with her in it. One of them told her, "'Woman, go out, or I will not teach!' Ironically, he was not even German, but Ukrainian!"[37]

Like other women of her social class, Regina volunteered for positions that allowed her to exercise her keen intellect, her sense of humor, and her leadership skills. She also had a talent for public speaking and, because of it, was elected president of the Sisterhood of B'nai B'rith. Her election was a major social honor: she was the first non-German-born woman to achieve this position, the highest social level of Jewish womanhood in Germany. Her reelection to a second consecutive term was unprecedented and a great social accomplishment.

On regular occasions, the Schaalmans hosted intellectual and artistic forums for Adolf's colleagues and artist friends. Because of his strong interest in the arts and the fact that he was so well respected for his astute critical judgment and support, Jewish artists, whom he had taken under his wing, frequently sought him out for advice and criticism.

Unlike Plaut's dispassionate and informal Jewish home life, Herman's was saturated in Judaism. It was intensely religious and joyful. The Schaalmans were Liberal Jews; in America, they practiced what would be considered Conservative Judaism. But in the Schaalman household, their observance was more strict and closer to those who were Orthodox. Schaalman's parents were masters at infusing Judaism with a sense of joy, making holiday celebrations, even High Holy Days, something to look forward to. This joy carried over to nonreligious celebrations, such as birthdays and wedding anniversaries.

Fundamental to the family's Judaism was the strict observance of Jewish dietary laws. The family never ate non-kosher food at any time or in any place. That restraint included not eating in restaurants to avoid the possibility that they might be served nonkosher food. His mother even made sure that when they went away for summer vacations they had enough kosher food to last the entire trip. Such an observant Jewish home life provided the future rabbi with "a fine Jewish upbringing and background...Because both my parents had a sense of aesthetics and style, their everyday life, including holidays and festivals, was tasteful and had its own beauty."[38]

After his bar mitzvah, Herman decided that he should be more observant. He made a commitment not to write on Shabbat, which meant that he could no longer attend the full six days of public school, Monday through Saturday. Because he was such a good student and his father was a professor, the school gave him permission to stay home on Shabbat.

Adolf, who was thoroughly competent in performing services for Shabbat and major holidays, volunteered as a lay *chazzan* (cantor) at a local orphanage, where he shared the responsibility of leading services with another volunteer cantor. The orphanage was connected to the *Liberale Gemeinde* (the branch of Liberal Judaism in Germany). Adolf considered it a mitzvah to provide services for the boys and girls who lived there. For Herman, the service, recited only in Hebrew, was beautiful, especially when the cantors sang together. His father knew all the melodies and traditional prayers for the entire year. On Rosh Hashanah and Yom Kippur, the cantors performed the entire service for the congregation. Adolf rehearsed for weeks before, and his sonorous and mellifluous voice could be heard throughout his apartment. Like his father, Herman had an outstanding singing voice and occasionally was called upon to chant prayers in the Munich synagogue.

Every Friday evening before dinner, Adolf and his sons attended services, either at the local synagogue or at the orphanage. Though the synagogue was more than a mile away, they always walked, and no matter what the weather, never considered using public transportation. Mrs. Schaalman remained at home to prepare the *Shabbos* meal.

This early idyllic life had a strong influence on Herman's decision to become a rabbi. He knew he wanted to help people and do something Jewish. His preparation for his bar mitzvah was key to his decision: "As a twelve-year-old, I was deeply affected by the experience. By the time I finished high school, I was convinced that the rabbinate was to be my life's work."[39]

His father was such a powerful role model that throughout Herman's adult life, he kept a picture of his father hanging next to his desk. Not a day passed when he didn't acknowledge him. Late in his life, Schaalman still evaluated his life in light of what he remembered were his father's values. His great disappointment was that his father did not live to experience some joy in his eldest son's achievements and that he didn't get the chance to solicit his father's opinion on issues important to him.

The Schaalman apartment on *Tengstrasse* gave them a bird's-eye view of the rise of the Nazi Party. In 1922, Munich became its first national headquarters and the home of Adolf Hitler. By leaning out his window, Herman could see Hitler and Goering drive up to the home of Franz Ritter von Epp, a Nazi who was an important nobleman and military officer. "I knew Hitler had arrived because wherever the car appeared, it was surrounded by a swarm of people."[40]

On another occasion when he was in high school and on his way home with a friend, Herman had a near run-in with the future Führer.

The two boys had stopped in at their favorite teahouse and were about to drink their tea when the door flew open. Eight SA men came in to case the room before Hitler walked in. Having no desire to be in the same room with him, before they were seen Herman and his friend snuck out the back door. On January 30, 1933, he had another encounter while he was on his way home from school and saw a large celebratory crowd assembled in front of Hitler's Munich headquarters. The event stuck in his memory because that was the day Hitler was installed as Germany's chancellor.

During these troubled times, Herman refused to be cowed by the Nazis and the rampant anti-Semitism around him. Because he was always either the smallest or the next-to-the-smallest kid in his class, he was an easy mark for the class bullies. Thanks to the fact that his father had hired a retired police officer to teach his son jujitsu, Herman, unlike his counterpart, Gunther Plaut, was not afraid to fight back. When attacked, he could defend himself. In one encounter in a locker room, when another boy said something disparaging and knocked him off a locker-room bench, Herman grabbed the bicycle chain he always brought to school and chased the boy to his home: "When I caught up with him, I beat the boy and then collapsed, possibly from the concussion that resulted when I fell off the locker room bench and hit my head on the concrete floor."[41]

To protect their children, some Jewish parents chose to remove them from school. Others denied they had any religious affiliation so they could qualify as a *Confessionslos*, a new, protected political class. Herman had a schoolmate whose parents declared themselves *Confessionslos*, though ultimately they still were victims of Nazi persecution. For the Schaalman family, such an option was inconceivable. They were proud of their Judaism. Banking on his military service, Adolf thought he was immune to the most drastic forms of persecution.

Another dramatic change occurred when students began wearing their Hitler Youth Movement uniforms to school. At the same time, when they assembled in the morning prior to the beginning of classes, the schools introduced a new ceremony: raising the Nazi flag. The ceremony was meant to demonstrate the power and authority the Nazis had over the education system. When the Nazi flag was raised for the first time in Herman's school, one of the tallest boys in his class accused him of slandering it. Herman had said nothing, but he knew he was in trouble.[42] While his teacher stood by helplessly, his accuser "pulled out his watch and said, 'I'll give you thirty seconds to retract what you have said or else I'll go to the Gestapo.'"[43] Schaalman didn't make a move. When the thirty seconds were up, the boy closed the watch and hauled off to belt his much smaller victim. Too late. The next moment, Schaalman used his jujitsu training to throw this attacker flat on his back. For the next two-and-a-half years of his schooling, no one dared to touch him.

In addition to the opening flag-raising ceremony that included giving the Nazi salute, Jewish pupils were forced to participate in compulsory racial-studies programs. Although this kind of harassment was endemic in the schools and meted out by both teachers and administrators, some of them were sympathetic and aware of the psychological and physical burden their Jewish students were experiencing. As time went on, however, in order to keep their jobs, more and more teachers sought to harass their Jewish students as a way of demonstrating their Nazi zeal.

Because the Nazis were obsessed by the worry that their pure Aryan blood might be polluted by the infusion of the blood of inferior races, they sent "experts" in physiognomy to the schools to lecture children on the dangers of associating with Jews, who were portrayed as lowlifes and criminals. The Nazis had developed the specious science of physical characteristics to identify an Aryan and a non-Aryan. A key measure was physiognomy. When specialists in the new science came to the schools, Jewish children were required to sit through virulent anti-Semitic propaganda while their classmates stared at them as models of the despised race. When one of these "experts" came to Herman's school to teach the students how to identify Jews, he picked Herman, a handsome, Aryan-looking youth as an example of the second-best racial type among the Germanic races. When his teacher whispered to this expert that Schaalman was the last Jewish student in the school, the expert fled the school and never returned.

Although the students were being propagandized to despise and reject Jews, they did not entirely reject Herman. Together with the school administration, they invited him to the high school graduation dance. Unwilling to give them the impression that he was afraid to go, Herman went with his Jewish girlfriend. They only stayed for one dance to show them he was not afraid.

Despite all the challenges he faced in the schools because he was a Jew, Herman's small size did not prevent him from participating in athletics. In fact, much like Plaut, he was an avid sportsman, though not at the same level. Remarkably, for a boy who was less than five feet tall, he was competent in high jumping, javelin, and discus. He was also an excellent swimmer and was fond of soccer and *Schlagball*, a variation of baseball, both highly competitive and physically demanding sports. His athletic ability made him one of the most sought-after boy in any game.

Herman's rigorous German education left an enduring mark on his development. He had begun school at the age of six and attended the neighborhood grade school for four years. When he was ten, his parents enrolled him in the *Gymnasium*, the German form of high school.

The nine years he spent there were preparation for admission to the university.

Although Herman was partially shielded from some of the anti-Semitism in his school, he could not avoid it in public places. On one occasion, he and his father—who thought of himself as the epitome of the Jewish stereotype with his dark hair and prominent nose—were riding on a streetcar. His father deliberately took out his Jewish newspaper and began to read it. Herman, who was sitting next to him, prepared himself to spring on the first attacker. Fortunately, no one bothered them. Adolf's deliberate provocation was based on his sense that he had a right to be who he was: after all, his family's roots went back to 1519 in Regensburg, and he had spent four and a half years in the trenches fighting for Germany.

Outside of school, Herman participated in youth-group activities. Not as daring as Plaut, Schaalman remembers that the first group he joined was the German-Jewish Boy Scouts, which he loved. He enjoyed the hiking, usually on Sundays, but did not participate in the summer camping activities because he accompanied his family on their summer vacations. As he got older, his teenage Jewish friends were drawn to political movements, particularly to Zionism, which had become a passion for many Jewish teenagers.

Some of Herman's friends became committed Zionists and immigrated to Palestine. Although Herman was sympathetic to Zionism, despite their best efforts, his friends could not convince him to go with them. Even if he had wanted to go, he would not have left his family, particularly his father. Like Jonas Plaut, Adolf tolerated his son's Zionist leanings but was not a Zionist himself.

Another group Herman joined was an educational group that studied the writings of Martin Buber, Germany's most famous Jewish scholar and intellectual. Sometimes, Buber even taught the course. For Schaalman, the experience of being in the presence of this great man was sufficient to leave a lasting mark on him and to become a major influence on his life.

These early experiences provided the grounding for the next phase of Herman's life. In the spring of 1935, he enrolled as a rabbinic student at the *Lehranstalt für die Wissenschaft des Judentums,* where he met the other members of the Gang of Five and began his journey to become a major leader in twentieth-century Reform Judaism.

WOLLI KAELTER

We feel the breadth of his prolific work...his cre-
ative and innovative programs
which serve as part of his legacy to Temple
Israel, his love of youth and camping
...his prophetic stance: fighting for civil rights,
[his advocacy] against the Viet Nam War
and for Gay and Lesbian rights—[and] hav-
ing the courage to call an injustice,
an injustice and the resolve to try and transform it into justice.
We feel his humanity, we feel his compassion, we feel his love,
we feel the way that he loved this precious gift of life.[44]
Rabbi Lee T. Bycel

In 1914, Wolfgang (Wolli) Kaelter was born into a distinguished rabbinic family in Danzig (now Gdansk), Poland. He was the fourth child
of Rabbi Robert Kaelter and his wife, Feodora. His music-loving parents
named him Wolfgang after Mozart and Goethe, although he later preferred to be called by his nickname, "Wolli."

In 1914, Danzig was a province of West Prussia, but by the end of
World War I, Danzig was granted free-city status through the Treaty
of Versailles and came under the protection of the newly established
League of Nations. The treaty recognized that the German majority in
the city did not want to be part of Poland.[45]

Wolli's father was not a conventional rabbi. Though Orthodox, he
defied the traditional rabbinic appearance of his day: no full-face beard
for him. Instead, he compromised with a Van Dyke. A more serious
rebellion was the fact that he dropped out of the traditional Orthodox-
leaning seminary in Breslau, Das Jüdisch-Theologische Seminar. His
alternative route was to be ordained by three other rabbis.

Rabbi Kaelter also defied the stereotype of the rigid and authoritarian father and rabbi. Wolli described him as fun-loving, humorous, and an enthusiastic outdoorsman. Like Schaalman's father, he made sacred time, such as Shabbat and the other Jewish holidays, a pleasant experience for his family. He also recognized the value of family outings. With his excellent sense of direction, he led them on Sunday hikes into the nearby forests.

One of Rabbi Kaelter's achievements that undoubtedly had a huge impact on Wolli was his untiring effort to provide comfort and support for the tens of thousands of Jewish refugees pouring into the city on their way to America and Canada. Because Danzig had been granted free-city status, it was a magnet for thousands of Russian and Polish Jews fleeing their homelands. The city had international protection and a free port without visa restrictions. Between 1920 and 1925, some sixty thousand Jews passed through the city. In these five years, its small Jewish community found itself facing the monumental task of caring for these refugees until their visas arrived from America or Canada.[46]

Together with the aid of two Jewish welfare agencies, the Joint Distribution Committee and HIAS, Rabbi Kaelter organized critical assistance for the refugees, many of whom were penniless. This immense task exacted a heavy toll and no doubt contributed to his early death. Although he was only fifty-one-years-old when he died in 1926, his work was known widely, and he was mourned by both German and Eastern European Jews. Because of this work and his loving relationship to his family, Rabbi Kaelter had a profound influence on Wolli: "I have never had any significant experience in my life since age twelve in which I have not felt the presence of my father."[47]

Rabbi Kaelter's sudden death came as a huge shock to his family, and it created a desperate financial hardship for his wife and their two younger sons who were still at home. Compounding their difficulties was the fact that Feo (short for Feodora) was subject to depression. As part of her effort to survive this crisis, she poured her energy into full-time volunteer work through which she helped find health care, food, clothing, and work for people who were unable to do so. Consequently, she became a major force for good in the Danzig community. For Wolli, however, there was a huge price to pay: she spent so much time in these activities and was absent so frequently that he got to know his nanny better than his mother.

Of Wolli's three other siblings, his sister, Ruth, the oldest, was her father's favorite. She combined brilliance with a passion for succeeding. At a time when it was unusual for a woman to pursue higher education, she earned a degree in philosophy from the University of Berlin. With this prestigious degree in hand, she made the daring choice to enroll in the famed Berlin seminary, the *Hochschule für die Wissenschaft des Judentums*, where Wolli would end up almost a decade later.

The second child, Franz, had little chance of competing with his sister. Because he was not as clever, he was a disappointment to his father, who was impatient with what he thought was his son's lack of ability. With a lowered set of expectations, Franz became a teacher in Saxony. The third child, Hans, took a different route than his older siblings. He turned his attention to labor issues and played a major role in founding the Danzig Jewish Workers Union.

At an early age, it must have been clear to anyone who was watching that Wolli was destined to be a rabbi. He loved to play with his tin soldiers, but unlike other boys, instead of having them shoot at each other, he conducted services and preached to them. He wrote, "I imagine I was imitating my father. No question my congregation was far more attentive than his."[48]

Wolli's early schooling began in a private school for upper-middle-class children. He was the only Jewish kid in his class and, like Plaut and Schaalman, found himself the butt of anti-Semitic attacks. When one of his gentile friends called him a Christ-killer, his father helped him understand that this charge wasn't true. The Jews, as subject people, could not have killed Christ; the Roman authorities killed him. When Wolli told his friend that he was wrong, the friend came back the next day with his Bible and showed Wolli the passage from the New Testament where the Jewish crowd chants, "Kill him, kill him!" Wolli learned from this experience that all that is printed is not necessarily true.

As older siblings, before they left home, Ruth and Franz thought they had an obligation to give Wolli his first private Hebrew lessons. But he was having none of it: "I was smart and wicked enough to always give the unexpected and undesired response…I had enough sense to know exactly what they wanted me to do or say and I didn't do or say it."[49] After their father died, they felt responsible for helping to raise him, if only by trying to educate him. Wolli's more official Hebrew lessons came from his father's assistant, Dr. David Weiss.

Before the Nazis came to power in 1933, rival political parties fought pitched battles in the streets of major German cities. Although not yet part of Germany, Danzig was no exception. Kaelter wrote, "You could never be sure that you wouldn't be a casual victim of the shooting."[50] This violence was never far from his home. On a Shabbat evening sometime in 1921, the Spartacists, who were in rebellion against the city government, fought a pitched battle with Danzig police right in front of the Kaelter home. Spartacists were holed up in a building across the street and were exchanging fire with the police. Anyone in the vicinity who had not taken cover was in mortal danger.

While this battle was taking place, Rabbi Kaelter was on his way home from Shabbat services at his synagogue. Somehow, he managed to get inside the house without getting hit by flying bullets. That night, the Kaelters ate their Shabbat dinner and conducted their Shabbat service in the hallway of their apartment, the only place without windows.

Wolli entered the *Gymnasium* when he was nine. Although the school was a municipal high school, his parents had to pay tuition, a hardship on a rabbi's salary. It was here that he began his formal music education and study of Latin, and later, Greek, German, mathematics, biology, geography, and history of both Germany and the world.

Although Wolli thought of himself as a good student (except for math), by the time he was fifteen, his grades were so poor that he was held back a year. School didn't agree with him, and he couldn't wait to get out: "With the exception of music and German literature...I disliked the methods of teaching, which I considered autocratic, pedantic, and unimaginative."[51] Part of what Wolli objected to was the memorization, a basic part of German education. Wolli, however, was good at it; he would memorize poems one day and forget them the next.

Although not sold on his schooling, he was excited in his pursuit of Jewish youth-group activities. His sister had already paved the way for him. She was a founding member of a group that became the Jung-Judischer Bund. Its goal was to develop the interest of young Jews in Jewish folklore, songs, history, art, and dramatics. The Bund had much in common with the German youth movement. As noted in our discussion of Plaut and Schaalman, because Jews were not accepted in the German youth movement, they formed their own groups. Not surprisingly, the young people of both groups were rebellious and took pleasure in violating the rules of their bourgeois and authoritarian parents and society. According to their parents' rules and their strictly held social norms, Jewish boys and girls did not go on hikes together or sleep out in shared tents or in farmers' barns. The members of the Jung-Judischer Bund had other ideas. Their rebellion against their parents and their society is an old story. The members of these youth groups accepted the criticism from their parents but considered it irrelevant.

For Wolli, as for so many other German-Jewish youths, the youth movement provided a vehicle for rebellion against what they thought was the assimilationist tendencies of their parents and grandparents. Many of the older generation were comfortable living as Germans and thought of themselves as Germans. Wolli's father, for example, was a committed patriot, convinced that German culture was supreme, superior to any other. In contrast, the young people felt a need to be closer to their Jewish roots: "Not only did they wish to rebel against their parents, but they were also very much aware of anti-Semitism, which was clearly alive in Germany."[52]

The Bund also provided its members with experiences they couldn't get in their segregated schools where boys and girls were separated. The Bund allowed them to comingle and socialize. Although not officially a Zionist group like those Plaut and Schaalman joined, the Bund shared many of the same goals. Its mission statement was a powerful affirmation of its function to provide social and intellectual experiences for its members and to create "a new type of Jew in Germany and in Europe generally."[53] Notable is the fact that, unlike the Zionist youth movement, the Bund's mission was not to encourage *aliyah*, but to shore up young people's Jewish identities as a bulwark against the onslaught of German and European anti-Semitism.

When Ruth passed on the office to Franz, the leadership of the group remained in the family. Franz moved the group in the direction of teaching its members a sense of responsibility for the "future of Judaism and the Jewish people." When he became too old to remain in the group, Wolli became his successor. Although he hated school, he loved the learning and camaraderie of the Bund. In his leadership role, he was responsible for planning weekly programs.

Many of the younger Bund members looked to him for fatherly advice. Although he was only a few years older, he provided advice and counseling to the fifteen- and sixteen-year-olds. Not all parents were pleased with this state of affairs and referred to him as "Hindenburg," the former general and president of Germany. The parents' sarcasm reflected their sense that this brash young man had too much influence over their children. No doubt these experiences were part of his preparation for his future role as rabbi and camp director.

Wolli's involvement in these all-consuming activities came at a price. If he had fallen behind in his schoolwork before, in this new leadership role, he neglected his homework completely. As noted above, the fifteen-year-old was held back for a year. (Imagine, the future rabbi failing in high school!) Unlike the other students, who customarily graduated at eighteen, he didn't graduate until he was twenty. Most importantly, his academic failure cost him his scholarship, creating a financial hardship for his mother, who was living off the limited pension of her deceased husband.

Like Plaut and Schaalman, Wolli met Martin Buber. He had already read Buber's *Reden über das Judentum* (1923), a collection of orations on Judaism and the future of Judaism.[54] Not long after, Buber spoke to Wolli's youth group, which was using Buber's writings as a source of serious study and discussion. Their study also included Rosenzweig and Baeck whom, along with Buber, were considered the three greatest Jewish intellectual and religious voices in contemporary Germany. As part of the group's education, they also studied Marx and Engels, whom they thought were Jews.

Kaelter's autobiography contains clues that he was sympathetic to extreme leftist politics. One of them was his special fondness for the book *Love and Death,* which he received in 1931 on his sixteenth birthday. The book contained letters written by left-wing radicals Karl Liebknecht and Rosa Luxemburg, the founders of Germany's Spartacist and Communist parties.[55] Strong opponents of Germany's decision to wage war, they advocated that workers unite to seize control of the corrupt capitalist system. In January 1919, the Communists in Berlin attempted a revolution, which was put down within a week. No mercy was shown to their leaders, who were murdered after being arrested. Luxemburg and Liebknecht, two of the most infamous, were apprehended and subsequently murdered by right-wing thugs.

When Hitler was elected premier in 1933, the Jewish community felt an almost immediate impact. The Nazis began issuing laws that affected Jews in ways large and small. One decree that had an immediate effect on Wolli was that Jews were no longer allowed to stay in youth hostels. For Wolli, who was a senior in the *Gymnasium*, this prohibition meant that he could not go on the class field trip. When he announced his intention to go anyway, a student wearing an SA uniform spoke up: "If Kaelter…cannot stay at the youth hostel, I have friends who will be glad to house him."[56] This support coming from a Nazi sympathizer must have come as a huge surprise. As it turned out, Wolli went on the trip and could stay with his class at the hostel.

Everyone in the Kaelter family expected that Wolli would become a rabbi. Very likely, his games with his toy soldiers had something to do with their expectations. He, however, had not made up his mind. In his diary, he wrote that he was still not sure what he was going to do with his life. He couldn't decide whether he wanted to become a social worker, a symphony conductor, an actor, or an opera singer. He was sure of one thing: "I want peace over the whole world. Music over the whole world. Laughter over the whole world. And Judaism as the great communicator of all this beauty."[57] He was also sure of his identity. He took his cue from his father, who identified himself as first a Jew and second a "*mensch*." Wolli wrote: "I would say, 'I am a mensch [and then] a Jew.'"[58]

As for the career as an opera singer, he discovered it would be more difficult than he imagined. When he was nineteen, he had his voice tested by one of the finest vocal coaches in Germany, a man called

Stueckgold. The coach was not impressed, however, and recommended a career as a cantor instead. Wolli decided to find out what such a career meant. In his interviews with four cantors, he discovered that they were frustrated and bitter about their jobs. Like him, they all began with the sense that their calling was opera, but their first disappointment was to find out that they couldn't make it. Their second choice of cantor as a fallback turned into another disillusionment when they realized that their congregations didn't appreciate the true quality of their voices. The cantors turned this disillusionment into contempt for their congregations. Wolli concluded that becoming a cantor was a bad choice. The only other option was to make use of his other talents and become a rabbi, a decision he made just prior to his twentieth birthday.

His next hurdle was high school graduation. He passed everything but math. The system allowed students to fail one subject and still graduate. The graduation ceremony, however, left a bad taste in his mouth. The graduates were to receive their certificates from the Nazi commissioner of education. Dressed in a Nazi uniform, he proceeded down the length of the graduation queue, handing out the certificates and shaking hands with the graduates. That is until he came to Wolli, whom he knew was a Jew. Neither wanted to shake the other's hand. The commissioner stopped in front of him and stared. Wolli stared back. The official nodded, Wolli nodded back, and the commissioner passed along to the next graduate. The year was 1934.

Following graduation from the *Gymnasium*, Wolli and his best friend, Bert Woythaler, left Danzig to enroll during the fall semester in Berlin's *Hochschule für die Wissenschaft des Judentums*. They discovered, however, that they didn't meet the school's entry standards for Jewish learning. After a semester of preparatory work, they were admitted to full-time study for the spring semester 1935.

Alfred Wolf

Alfred Wolf's contributions to Reform Judaism en-
compassed "every phase and function
of the American synagogue." [59]
Rabbi Samson H. Levey

When Alfred Wolf was born on October 7, 1915, World War I was already raging in Europe. Like Schaalman's father, Alfred's father, Herman, who had been drafted at the age of eighteen, was serving in an artillery detachment at the front. He had been called up almost as soon as he and his fiancée, Regine, were married in July 1914. While on their way to their honeymoon, he received notice that he had been drafted. Alfred speculates that his father must have come home on leave in early February 1915, because he was born nine months later. Herman didn't come home again until he was discharged in either late 1918 or early 1919. One of Wolf's earliest memories was of his father coming home from the war dressed in a dirty uniform and wearing what he described as a "grizzled" beard. To the three-year-old, the stranger was an alien presence. "'I want that man to go away!'"[60] the child screamed. But Herman didn't, and he and Alfred soon found that the they became "good friends."

In his autobiography, Wolf wrote that "Alfred" was not a typical German name but was English. When his mother decided on the name, she was sharply criticized by her neighbors. How could she use an English name when her husband was away fighting the English on the Western Front?

Alfred was fortunate to be born into the most prominent family in Eberbach, a small town of approximately seven thousand located near Frankfurt and Heidelberg. Founded in 1227, it had a proud history and strong traditions, and neighborliness was one of them. For a substantial core of the population, being a neighbor meant a great deal, enough that one would risk one's neck to smuggle food to a Jewish neighbor who was no longer permitted to buy food under the new Nazi rules. Consequently, Wolf wrote, for the handful of Jewish families living in Eberbach, life was otherwise mostly tolerable.

Germany's huge inflation proved to be a serious problem for the Wolf family, as it was for everyone else. The value of the mark plummeted quickly. Every day, when word of the new value was posted, store owners immediately recalculated their prices. Because of food shortages, the government was forced to institute rationing. Based on the number of people in a family, each household was issued a ration book that allowed them to purchase necessities such as milk, bread, meat, and a few major foods. People, however, found ways around the system. Whether you could get food often depended on your relationship with the seller: "If you were not on the butcher's list of preferred customers you might find out through the grapevine that 'yesterday they had some excellent beef.'"[61]

Alfred's father tried to cope with the changes by taking the train to Mannheim to buy necessities, fifty kilometers away. A window of opportunity existed between 3:00 and 4:00 a.m., just before the new money values were posted! If Herman didn't get there during this time, he couldn't afford to pay the wholesale prices of the next day: "Failure to beat that key moment could be a first step toward bankruptcy."[62]

The best method of getting food was through connections with the farmers who provided it to the butchers and grocery stores. In this, the Wolfs, who owned and operated a successful dry goods store, had an advantage: many of their regular customers were farmers and owners of cattle and chickens. Although sales that bypassed the rationing system were illegal, people were willing to subvert the system. Good customers of the Wolfs would sell them items at a higher price than they could get commercially, or they would engage in a quid pro quo of buying from the Wolfs at a substantial discount.

Sometimes the Wolfs would set out on a ten-mile hike to the village of Sensbach to buy what they could "from a trustworthy peasant." They would go at night to avoid detection by the authorities and return "on a narrow footpath" so that they were not likely to be seen. Because he loved hiking, Alfred enjoyed these adventures with his family.

Being Jewish in Germany, however, meant that life—even before Hitler—was not easy. The issues of German nationalism and anti-Semitism stood in the way. Nationalism was instilled in German children both from their families and their schools. They grew up knowing that their history and bloodlines went back hundreds, if not thousands of years, and that their ancestors fought Caesar and his Roman armies, and contributed to the fall of the Roman Empire. No matter how hard they tried, Jewish children could never have this identification. In their own eyes and in the eyes of other Germans, they were aliens. The history of Jews in Europe was a history of pogroms and statelessness.

The problem for Alfred and the few other Jewish children in town was that they could not make friends with the other non-Jewish children. Nor was it possible for Alfred to make friends with the four Jewish children. Two boys were too old for him and soon left to take jobs in a larger city. The other Jewish children, a boy and his even younger sister, were too young for him.

By the early 1920s, Alfred began to learn about the Nazi threat. Although he was too young to know what it meant, he knew from his elders that Hitler was an evil man who did not like Jews and who wore a funny uniform. In the early days, even though he was ridiculed elsewhere, Hitler was having an impact on Eberbach: The manager of the largest factory in Eberbach was one of Hitler's early supporters, and when Hitler needed money, which was an ongoing problem, he was a frequent visitor. The manager was so pro-Nazi that to get a job in his factory meant you had to be either SA or SS."

In his years in primary school (fifth to eleventh grades), Alfred was the top student in his class. For seven years, he earned the prestigious title of "primus," a status that entitled him to receive a special book award. When Hitler came to power, one of the teachers in the school, a self-declared Nazi, objected to a Jew receiving this honor. The issue was settled by the principal, a liberal democrat, who proposed a compromise: Alfred could receive the honor of primus but would not get the book.

While in primary school, Alfred was the victim of an anti-Semitic insult. Once the Nazis began to assert control, one of the students called him "a dirty Jew." Alfred reported the incident to the principal, who gave the offending child a warning. Once the Nazis were in firm control, the principal was transferred to a job as a classroom teacher in a school thirty miles away.

The schools kept records of their students' religion and provided two hours each week in religious instruction for Protestant and Catholic students. Since Alfred was the only Jewish student in the school, he could get his religious instruction through his synagogue or, more often, in the home of Mr. Frohmann, who served his fellow Jews in various roles: teacher-cantor-*shokhet* (slaughterer)-"marrier and burier" for Eberbach and surrounding towns and villages.

When Alfred turned six, he began his Jewish studies with Frohmann, who, together with Alfred's grandfather, Benjamin Levy, were the two most influential forces in his decision to become a rabbi. While his grandfather was alive and well, Alfred went to his apartment several times a week to study with him for an hour or more. Frohmann gave him a well-rounded Orthodox education, including training in how to conduct services.

Alfred must have been quite capable as a student of Hebrew because, even before his bar mitzvah, he was called to the bimah to chant the

Haftorah on Shabbat and festivals. Like Schaalman, he could chant the Hebrew text on sight and without practice. Not only could he sight-read, but he knew the musical notation (cantillation) and could chant major portions of the service. Once he had his bar mitzvah, he and his grandfather led the services. When there was no *minyan*, his job was to knock on doors to get additional men to make the ten-member minyan requirement.

When Alfred was in his twelfth and thirteenth years in school, he became a "volunteer" youth leader in Heidelberg, twenty miles from Eberbach. He took advantage of the situation to take private lessons in advanced Hebrew studies from Dr. Pinkuss, a local rabbi. His study with Pinkuss satisfied his school requirement that he take two hours of weekly religious instruction. Wolf wasn't sure Pinkuss liked the extra work, but he appreciated Alfred's efforts to organize and lead a group of teenage boys in his congregation. Once the Nazis took control and Jewish youths were excluded from official German youth groups, these teens would have been at loose ends without Alfred's efforts.

Although Frohmann and Levy had been early influences on Alfred's decision to become a rabbi, Rabbi Pinkuss put the icing on the cake. It was Pinkuss who asked him what he wanted to do for his future career. Before Alfred could tell him, Pinkuss took out a piece of paper and wrote something on it and then turned it face down. Once Alfred told him what he wanted to be, Pinkuss turned the paper right side up. It read "RABBI."

Although Heidelberg had a small Jewish community of about a hundred families, it needed a teenage leader for its boys and girls.[63] Alfred got his early training as a youth leader by taking on the responsibility of organizing and leading them. Although he was already making two-hour round trips to Heidelberg five days a week, he volunteered to travel another day most weekends to conduct a late-afternoon or evening event for his boys' group. Many years later, he was surprised when he realized that the boys' parents had "no hesitancy to entrust their children to 'that boy from Eberbach.'"[64]

As the group leader, Alfred arranged weekly group sessions and hikes both local and distant, including a week-long hike through the Black Forest. He knew the potential danger for a young Jewish boy to be out alone so late at night. It was a time when no Jew could feel secure at any time from an attack by SA, SS, or even Hitler Youth. He knew that Nazi hoodlums were always on the prowl, especially eager to taunt and attack Jews. Why did he take such chances not just for himself but for his boys? In his "Memories," Wolf speculated that his motivation might have come from a sense of duty, a feeling of responsibility to do something necessary that nobody else was willing to tackle, and a daredevil act by one unwilling to admit to the dangers to which he exposed himself and his charges. He and the boys, however, came through these experiences without difficulty: "God must have approved of what I was doing. Nothing ever happened to 'my boys.'"[65]

Like so many of Germany's Jews, including Schaalman's and Plaut's fathers, Alfred's father was convinced that Hitler could never last. So confident was he that he placed a bet with his brother that Hitler would be out in months. This was not an unreasonable bet. The chancellorship had been a swinging door during the months prior to Hitler's election. He had come to power with the support of powerful industrialists: "They counted on him to keep the working class in line and from joining the leftist parties, notably the Social Democrats who were very powerful in the Reichstag."[66] Nonetheless, Herman took an active role in fighting the Nazis. He marched with the Reichsbanner, a militia sponsored by the Social Democratic and the Democratic Parties. These marches were often attacked by the SA and SS.

Alfred's opportunities to associate with and date Jewish girls were limited. The only Jewish girl in his hometown was too young for him. To find a few girls nearly his own age, he had to travel to Neckarsteinach, a small town halfway between Eberbach and Heidelberg.

Under such circumstances the question of intermarriage, at least theoretically, was a real concern. Had he chosen to marry a non-Jew, he would not have been the first in his family to do so. Before the Nazi takeover, intermarriage had been rampant in Germany. According to Marion Kaplan, by 1927, 25 percent of Jewish men and 16 percent of Jewish women had married outside their religion. Most of the children of intermarriage were raised as Christians, some learning of their Jewish lineage only after 1933. In the large cities, marriage to Christians was becoming so common—especially among Jewish men—that some Jewish leaders feared the complete fusion of their community into German society by the end of the twentieth century. [67]

Ties to traditional Judaism began to erode during the nineteenth century, when the Enlightenment allowed German Jews more freedom, not only to be Jewish but German as well. Assimilation was now a goal of many German Jews who wanted out of the ghetto and acceptance for their talents and abilities in the larger social world. [68] However, second- and third-generation Germans discovered to their horror that under the new Nazi laws, they were Jews and that their intermarriages were illegal. [69]

Once the Nazis took over, Alfred's family business began to suffer. Most of their customers were non-Jews, and when the Nazi order of *Kauft Nicht Beim Juden* ("don't buy anything from Jews") was enacted, they stopped coming. Some customers remained faithful to their Jewish friends. Others, who needed essential items, continued to patronize the store. Although their business suffered badly, the Wolfs did not go hungry. They could hold out until 1940, when they were forced to sell their business and were deported to the Gurs concentration camp in Vichy, France.

The Wolfs were fortunate to have a protector, a local police chief who was the father of Alfred's best friend, Alfred Fleitz. During the Nazi terror, the chief ran interference for the family. Shortly after the Nazis took power in 1933, Fleitz, dressed in civilian clothes, came to

Alfred's home to warn his parents that the local Nazis were planning a "spontaneous popular protest" against them. If they were at home at the time, he would have to take them into protective custody and put them in jail. To avoid this situation, he suggested that they leave town to visit relatives. Once they left, he promised that he would not consider it his duty to pursue them.

The Wolfs decided to visit relatives in Auerbach, which was not far from Heidelberg. By coincidence, Alfred's high school class had arranged a trip that day to Heidelberg to see a performance of Shakespeare's *The Merchant of Venice*. At the end of the play, he rushed to make the last train back to Eberbach, only to find his parents waiting for him at the Heidelberg station. They told him that police chief Fleitz had warned them that if they didn't get out of the city, he would have to arrest them. They wanted Alfred to know that they were on their way to visit relatives in nearby Auerbach and had arranged for their chauffeur to meet him at the Eberbach station and take him to his grandparents' home, where he would be safe.

In the spring of 1935, Alfred enrolled in the *Lehranstalt für die Wissenschaft des Judentums*, where he met up with the other members of the Gang of Five.

Leo Lichtenberg

> *My father was a humble man. He lived mod-*
> *estly and toiled in the fields*
> *of college youth throughout his career. He felt*
> *strongly about keeping young people*
> *in the fold, especially in response to the holocaust. He felt, therefore,*
> *that we should never close our doors to those young people*
> *who wanted to marry non-Jews. Dad*
> *was the only rabbi in the area*
> *who would perform intermarriages: "Why lose one," he would ask,*
> *"when I may gain two?"*
>
> Ruth Levor, daughter of Rabbi Lichtenberg

Leo was born in 1915 in Rostock to parents Leo and Lucy (Stern) Lichtenberg. He never knew his father, who died before he was born. Because his mother was still pregnant when her husband died, she decided to name their son Leo after his father. Although legally blind and poor, Lucy somehow managed to raise her son under extremely difficult circumstances. From the time he was a child, Leo—like Schaalman, Kaelter, and Wolf—knew he wanted to become a rabbi.

Sometime during his youth, his mother moved to Berlin to be close to her family. The family was very supportive, helped with money, and sent Leo to camp. After finishing secondary school in 1935, Leo enrolled in the *Lehranstalt für die Wissenschaft des Judentums* to fulfill his desire to become a rabbi. When he was selected to receive one of the five scholarships offered by Hebrew Union College, he ran into a problem: because he had no family in the United States, he needed an affidavit to enter. Fortunately, a Cincinnati-based social-service agency came to his rescue and contacted a local resident, Jacob Mack, who provided the affidavit.

The members of the Gang of Five were now assembled and ready for their new adventure. It was a fateful decision that would mold the rest of their lives

W. Gunther Plaut

Herman E. Schaalman

Wolli Kaelter

Alfred Wolf

Leo Lichtenberg

PART 3

Studying to Be a Rabbi

DEPARTURE FOR AMERICA

BY LEAVING GERMANY, THESE YOUNG refugee students left behind their culture, their religious views and practices, and their families. They also left a country with a cultural heritage that was the envy of the Western world. The rabbinic students' decision to leave their homeland was an act of courage and foresight. Had they not left when they did, they might never have been heard from again. Yet, they had no idea how lucky they were to get out of Germany when they did. They fully expected to return and lead normal lives once the Nazi period came to an end. In that, they shared the all-too-common perspective of many German Jews, who could not believe that catastrophe was just around the corner.

In 1935, getting a student visa to the United States was easy; the Nazis were only too cooperative. A month after the scholarship students were selected, they began their journey to America. They left just shortly before the Nuremberg Laws were enacted on September 15, 1935. Among their various provisions, the new laws denied German Jews their citizenship. The students' plan, according to Schaalman, was to meet in Paris and then on to Le Havre, where they would board the *Brittanic*. They expected to arrive in New York the day before Labor Day, September 5, 1935.

On their arrival, Plaut, Wolf, and Schaalman were met by relatives, but not Kaelter and Lichtenberg. Kaelter was bitter because he thought he deserved better: "My father had helped 65,000 Jews to come to America and not one of them was there to meet me?"[70] Of course, he realized that no one knew he was coming and that his petulance was totally irrational.

For this group of European students, the arrival in New York Harbor was a cultural awakening. Wolf described it this way:

> To a European who had seen New York's skyline only in movies or still pictures and for whom one of the very few twenty- or thirty-story buildings in places like Berlin or Hamburg were exceptionally tall structures, the actual view of New York approaching from the ocean and steaming into the harbor has to be an emotional experience. In Europe, the Eiffel Tower is literally a unique experience, but part of is [sic] uniqueness is its standing completely alone on the vast skyline of Paris. And you know that it was built as part of an exhibit and that nobody lives or runs a business there. New York, on the other hand, is a city. People live in those buildings, work in those buildings. It's unique![71]

To learn more about America, HUC had arranged that on their way to Cincinnati they would take a detour and make a brief visit to the nation's capital. After a one-day visit, they traveled overnight on a B & O train to Cincinnati. The journey turned out to be an unexpected delight. Schaalman explained that, although he had ridden on trains in Germany, he was not used to riding in luxury. The coach class, where he was sitting on his way to Cincinnati, had upholstered seats. In Germany, coach meant you sat on wooden benches, the only way the Schaalmans could afford to travel. On this trip, his cushioned seats were the equivalent of second class, which was more luxurious than coach.

Because they knew little about America and even less about American Reform Judaism, their first impressions reinforced the negative stereotypes they brought with them.[72] When they arrived in Cincinnati, Professor Nelson Glueck, HUC professor of Bible, who would later become famous as an archaeologist and president of HUC, was supposed to meet them at the train. Because the students were guests of HUC, they expected to be picked up promptly. Wolf put it this way: "We got off the train and waited…Soon we were the only ones by the tracks except for a young man [actually Professor Glueck] who approached us reluctantly and said, in fairly good German, 'Are you the five students from Berlin?'"[73]

Schaalman reported that Glueck took them to breakfast at the home of his mother-in-law, Mrs. Ranshoff, the daughter of a prominent Cincinnati family.[74] Their breakfast consisted of bacon and eggs, food that was totally foreign to them and a major violation of their kosher upbringing. Even though the students were famished, Plaut, speaking for the rest of them, told their hosts that they were not hungry and had already eaten. When Glueck realized that none of them would eat nonkosher food, he was mortified and immediately ordered that the food be taken away. Schaalman added: "The food that was served next was either new eggs without the bacon or the old eggs with the bacon removed from their plates."[75] Not wanting to offend their hosts, they ate the food.

At first, the young refugees had difficulty adjusting to this new religious world and to American customs and values. According to Schaalman:

We saw ourselves as coming to a new world that called on us to radically reshape our entire existence. It is the Promised Land full of hope and opportunity for individual prosperity and happiness. We had to adapt to this new world in ways we could not have imagined. Intellectually and emotionally, this radical adjustment was confusing and disorienting.[76]

The refugee students had a harder time adjusting to the ways of American Reform Judaism. On the second day after they arrived at HUC, they ran smack into the wall of Classical Reform. It was Shabbat, and Rabbi David Philipson, one of the foremost rabbinic scholars of his time and a teacher at HUC, invited them to attend services at his temple in Rockdale, a Cincinnati neighborhood.

According to Kaelter, Philipson's assistant, Rabbi Morton Cohen, dispatched his wife to pick them up. Behind the wheel of a flashy car with the radio blaring, they saw "a buxom blonde who looked like Jean Harlow...in short skirts" who was not much older than the students themselves. Plaut wrote that he did not "know a single rabbi who had a car, let alone a *rebbetzin* who would be allowed to drive one."[77] Schaalman was similarly impressed.

When she got out of the car, she introduced herself as Sally Cohen, wife of Rabbi Cohen, who had come to drive them to the temple. Although none of the young men had ever ridden to Shabbat services, as captives of their new surroundings, they got in the car and drove off with her. Sensing their embarrassment, Sally reacted, "When in Rome, do as the Romans do."[78] She was probably just as surprised and amused by the students' appearance. They were dressed in their formal German synagogue clothes, replete with their broad-brimmed hats. (According to Schaalman, no respectable German Jew would be seen in a German synagogue without a top hat.)

When the students arrived at the temple, an usher escorted them to the front row of a nearly empty sanctuary. As was customary in a Liberal synagogue, men and women were seated together. This new fact of life took the students by surprise. In Germany, synagogues were packed and served as the center of Jewish life.[79] The prayer books were another surprise. Largely in English, the thin books opened from left to right. Another surprise for Plaut was that the two men sitting on the bimah in black robes were not the rabbi and the cantor. One was the famous Rabbi David Philipson; the other was his assistant, Rabbi Morton Cohen. Neither wore a kippah or prayer shawl, and they conducted the service almost entirely in English. It was also apparent that most of the congregation knew next to no Hebrew. The students had entered the strange new world of American Reform Judaism.

In the meantime, Philipson had his own issues with the greenhorns. He was seventy-three years old and had been serving as Rockdale Temple's rabbi for the last forty-seven years. As a founding member of the Central Conference of American Rabbis and its president from 1907 to 1909, he was regarded as a leader of Classical Reform Judaism. He was also a staunch advocate of Americanism, which meant that he had devoted his life to the assimilation of Jews into American life.[80] He was in no mood to tolerate the students' outlandish attire.

Philipson had a clear view of the refugees and became increasingly irritated as the service proceeded. Kaelter described him as "close to apoplexy." The custom of wearing hats in a Reform service was strictly taboo. As Kaelter tells it, "he could barely get through the Kaddish before summoning us to his study."[81] In Plaut's account, Philipson "glowered" at them and in "stentorian tones well within the hearing of the other congregants" ushered them into his study and demanded to know why they did not remove their hats.[82]

"The first thing you have to learn," he reprimanded them, "is manners. In our temple we have long given up the wearing of hats." Then he turned nasty: "If you ever appear here again with those things on your heads, I will have you physically removed."[83] Plaut speculated that to Philipson, "the chief exponent of [Reform's] classical expression," the immigrants must have represented "the antithesis of his ideals." With their butchered English, they must have reminded Philipson of the Old World from which Reform Judaism had tried to distance itself.

In their attempt to defend themselves, the students told him that they had cleared wearing hats with HUC's president, Dr. Julian Morgenstern. Philipson was not mollified; Morgenstern might have given them permission to wear their hats during services at HUC, but not in Rockdale.

In separate accounts of the incident, Schaalman and Kaelter reported that when they objected, Philipson gave them the same response as Sally Cohen: "When in Rome, do as the Romans do." Schaalman, the brash and quick-witted youngest member of the group, fired back, "I thought we were in Cincinnati."[84] Plaut vowed that he would never "set foot in Rockdale Temple again as long as Dr. Philipson was the rabbi."

Soon after their arrival at HUC, the students attended their first High Holy Day services. The experience was a real eye-opener. Held in Cincinnati's famed Plum Street Temple, the synagogue was crammed wall to wall. According to Kaelter, the entire service was conducted in English, and the women were dressed in "party-like" dresses that were "too showy, too extravagant." He also objected to the music, which sounded "totally goyish"; he couldn't recognize a single tune. [85] The sermon proved to be another obstacle for the new students. Kaelter reported that not only could he not understand it, but he was so distraught that he left the service "in tears and vowed never to return or to participate in such a service." Ironically, he did return many years later to give the ordination speech to the 1985 graduating seniors. Schaalman also returned to give the ordination speech to the graduating class of 2007.

HEBREW UNION COLLEGE: 1935–1941

In 1935, Hebrew Union College was a very small seminary with an enrollment of sixty students. Having been built in the 1920s, it was relatively new. In comparison to the modest building of their Berlin seminary, which, according to Plaut, was located in "squalid surroundings," the college was "unreal in its splendor and extravagance…a series of castles set in spacious grounds."[86] For Plaut, this was a reflection of American opulence.

In addition to an administration building, which housed the classrooms, the complex included a dormitory, gymnasium, swimming pool, and two outdoor tennis courts. HUC provided the refugees full financial aid, including tuition, room and board, and all fees. This beneficence was part of an "ancient custom" of relieving aspiring scholars of financial worries, a practice even for scholars in European *shtetls* and one that had been transplanted to America.

Because the Nazis had devastated their families' financial resources, the young men would not have been able to accept the scholarships without financial assistance. When the students arrived without any money, the college gave them a loan of twenty dollars, which they were required to repay when they left the college. In order to repay the loan and to have some spending money for himself, Schaalman worked ten hours a week for a professor, who paid him five dollars a week.

When the students arrived, the seminary was strictly a male institution. The only women on campus were two secretaries, two cooks, and Lillian Waldman, the dorm matron. Plaut and Schaalman were extremely fond of her. Schaalman described her as a "wise, gentle, [and] charming" woman who also served as a surrogate mother [and a good sounding board. Because I was far from home and parents and utterly alone, I confided in her and asked questions I could never ask anybody else."[87]

Schaalman was not the only one feeling isolated and alone. Plaut wrote that the refugee students felt "rootless" and like aliens in a strange new land. They compensated for this feeling by sticking together and creating a fraternity with a common language and culture, a group within which they could share memories and stories of their past lives. They found comfort in their teachers, most of whom had been educated in Germany and spoke fluent German.

Compounding their adjustment difficulties was their growing awareness of what was happening in Germany and the danger these events posed to their parents and families. Although they did not know about the horrors the Nazis were perpetrating against Jews, the cables they received made them anxious about the safety of their families. Nonetheless, even when the war broke out in Europe in 1939, they were so removed that, according to Schaalman, "They did not feel engaged... We felt protected and sheltered from the world."[88]

Another of the profound transformations the students had to make was to their cultural stereotypes of America. Traditional Judaism frowns on hunting or any other activity that causes pain to living creatures. The Jews Schaalman knew in Germany did not own guns or hunt or fish; the few Jews who did were the exception. When one of his HUC fellow rabbinic students brought out a gun and boasted about its use, Schaalman was surprised and put off.

Americans, unlike Germans, gave their children middle names. In his effort to adapt to the customs of his new country, Schaalman adopted his Hebrew name, "Ezra," as his middle name, the Hebrew name he had been given to perpetuate the memory of his maternal grandfather, "Ernst Ezra." He changed the spelling of his last name. Soon after his arrival in America, he was advised to use an American spelling, which required that he drop the double "n" from Schaalmann.

In practical terms, the culture of Reform Judaism was embodied by the HUC president, Dr. Julian Morgenstern, its faculty, and its students. Morgenstern had never attended a Passover Seder until he was ordained in 1902. Even after that, he was not observant and always felt slightly uncomfortable in traditional Jewish settings. His minimalist ritual practice was also the practice of most of the faculty, and nearly all of the students. A handful of the faculty and students were Shabbat observant or kept kosher. Because Classical Reform had banned the wearing of yarmulkes and *tallit*, services in the HUC chapel were conducted without head covering or prayer shawls. Most of the students only came to Shabbat morning services when attendance was required, and they rarely came to the daily services.

Not all the adjustments the refugee students had to make to their new lives were problematic. As students in the Berlin seminary, they had been responsible for finding their own housing and providing for their own meals. At HUC, room and board, including all meals, were provided. The food, however, was a problem. As Schaalman explains, and he might well have been speaking for all of them: "Because I had been brought up in a strictly kosher home, the thought of eating non-kosher food was at first repugnant, though later it proved to be liberating."[89] Another issue for the young students was that, although HUC did not serve pork or shellfish, it did not observe the commandment to keep milk and meat separate.

More astonishing for Schaalman was the fact that he did not have to clean up after himself. An African American man, the first he had ever met, showed up every day to make his bed and clean his room. All the other service jobs in the college were performed by African Americans. Although these amenities were 'foreign' at first, he soon got used to them; he felt as though he were living in a 'Never Never Land.'

Not only were the customs strange, but because Schaalman had not mastered the language, trouble started on his second day when he found himself the butt of an upperclassman's practical joke. When Herman's dorm matron invited him to introduce himself to a group of women visiting the college, he readily accepted. The upperclassman, however, exploiting the fact that Schaalman knew very little English, told him to address the women with a word that Schaalman later learned was "foul and sexually perverted." When he greeted the women with the word, they turned all shades of red and looked very uncomfortable. Schaalman has never revealed the word: "The episode was so demeaning that I have never used the word again."[90]

Newspapers also proved to be a challenge for the students. When Schaalman read a headline on the sports page, "Webber died on third," he wondered what it might mean. What was "third"? Who was Webber? How did he die? Learning English was a continuing challenge. Plaut relates a similar experience. The headline of the Cincinnati paper read: "REDS MURDER CARDINALS." He thought that it meant "the revolution had come to Rome."[91] In time, Schaalman claimed that his command of German began to slip: "Now my German is street German, but my vocabulary for curses remains strong, particularly Bavarian curses." Referring to his friends, he says, "We were really masters, experts in swearing."[92]

Schaalman's experience with the challenges of English was not unique. Kaelter relates one of his comical experiences involving a mix-up of English words. Lillian Waldman had discovered him in the hall with a pocketbook he had taken from a young woman who was visiting a friend. He took the purse as a joke, but when Waldman confronted him, he said, "Oh, Mrs. Waldman, I just raped her." He intended to say "I just robbed her. When I discovered my error, I was so mortified that I hid in my room for the next two hours."[93]

At first, the refugee students were not well received by the other students. Kaelter described them as "suspicious and standoffish." Plaut thought that at first, they were "leery." "This response," Schaalman added, "was based, in part, on their perception that we huddled together to talk about them in German and because we introduced rituals (such as the *birkat hamazon*) in the dining hall that were not part of the seminary's practice."[94] It is quite likely that their perceived clannishness and their attempts at reforming ritualistic practices moved some of their classmates to label them "the Gang of Five."

Fortunately, a group of eight or ten classmates with similar religious beliefs formed a support group for the refugees. Kaelter identifies them as Lou H. Silberman, Myron Silverman, Dudley Weinberg, Morton Fierman, Malcolm Stern, Bernie Rosenberg, Abe Shaw, and David Schor. Schaalman described them as "sensitive," "gentle," and "understanding." "They helped us learn English and served as a buffer against other students who might otherwise have made fun of us."[95] Plaut described Weinberg as "one of the most sensitive and beautiful human beings it has ever been my privilege to know."[96] Kaelter wrote that because Silberman befriended the Germans, he became known to his American classmates as the "sixth German."

Despite the best efforts of their friends, some unfortunate incidents did occur. A classmate, whom Schaalman declined to identify, referred to the Germans as "Heinies," a derogatory term coined during World War I: "He never spoke of anything else and enjoyed announcing when they arrived at an event, 'The Heinies are here,' or 'Hi, Heinies.'"[97] Although spoken in jest, the Germans sensed an insult.

Like their German immigrant students, many HUC faculty members were also foreigners who had had to learn English when they arrived in America. Most were largely sympathetic, but not all. A few who were wedded to the school of biblical criticism thought the Germans were not convinced that HUC's methods and conclusions were valid. Schaalman believed that these faculty members were frustrated because they didn't get the enthusiastic response they desired: "When it did not happen, they chose to ignore us."[98]

One of the immediate challenges the refugee students faced was an entrance examination. According to Kaelter, "The news really shook the five of us." Why would such tests be necessary when so many of the HUC faculty had studied at the *Hochschule*? Because the refugee students considered Hebrew Union College inferior to their Berlin seminary, they had expected that shortly they would be asked to teach in the institution, but when that didn't happen, they were rudely disappointed. In their second week, they were told they had to enroll at the University of Cincinnati to earn undergraduate degrees. Although they did not know it at the time, they were not singled out as exceptions: some of the American-born students entering HUC had come directly from high school and were required to get an undergraduate degree from the university while at the same time pursuing a BA from HUC.

The five refugee students were advised to make the rounds of the various academic departments of the University of Cincinnati to find a major that would accept them and whether any of their prior education could be parlayed into sufficient credits to earn a degree. They all majored in German. When they found themselves in a class with a professor who had a PhD in German from Yale but who knew very little, they drove him crazy. The professor retaliated by putting them in a separate group and assigning them to read second rate and boring German literature that they had managed to escape in Germany. Kaelter described the literature as "junk," but they had to read a "mind boggling" amount of it to complete their major. Although he had never earned anything less than an A in German in Germany, Kaelter now found himself with a B in Cincinnati.

Another professor named Diesendruck also became the butt of the Gang's pranks. When they discovered that he could easily be derailed from the course of his lecture, they would ask him totally unrelated questions. Schaalman described the game they played with him as "football." Before class, they would take turns making up questions to absolutely be sure to distract him from teaching philosophy. They always succeeded, and these digressions frequently monopolized the entire class time. They asked him inane questions such as "why the Cincinnati Reds would not win the pennant this year? Or why the French had negotiated with the Nazis who had defeated them?"[99]

HUC provided the "Gang" its own set of challenges. Reform ritual practice was the first hurdle. So novel were the Reform practices of the day that Schaalman called them "a revolution," to which he needed to adjust. One example was the wearing of a *kippah*. When he chanted in the choir at the college, he felt "naked" without it. His training told him he was sinning against God, yet the administration chastised him when he wore it. *Davening* without a *kippah* was not only an issue for Schaalman, but also for his immigrant colleagues. Plaut wrote that none of them had ever davened without one, nor, at first, could they conceive of doing so. By the time of their ordinations, however, except for Kaelter, the other students had given up wearing them.

For Schaalman, this experience was a major event in his religious life. From that time forward, he knew that God was much too busy to be concerned with such little things as a *kippah*. This Reform practice, so different from what the students knew, helped prepare them to accept the ideological foundation of Reform Judaism. The key to that understanding was the importance of critical thinking. They learned to apply reason as a test for the validity of ritual and liturgical practice. Schaalman concluded that reason is one of God's great endowments and gifts.

The young rabbinic students had to make other adjustments at HUC. In Germany, prayers were recited in Hebrew, whether one knew the meaning or not. In contrast, Reform Judaism chose to use English translations so that congregants could understand the prayers they were chanting. Not only did the Gang have difficulty understanding the English translations, but they also recognized that the translations lacked the sense of ritual language they were used to.

Because they came from more traditional religious backgrounds and very different cultural experiences, the five refugee students found that they ran headlong into a clash of cultures and religious practices at HUC. As noted previously, at first they wore *kippahs* to services and chanted the complete *birkat hamazon* alone. Reciting the *birkat*, laying on of *tefillin*, and the wearing a *kippah* were all part of the traditional practices the young men brought with them. When Schaalman attempted to introduce the *birkat* at the end of a meal in the student cafeteria, the students jeered them and then got up and left the room. Many years later, Schaalman thought that the students very likely were offended not by the practice, but by their perception that these foreigners were attempting to impose our own religious practices on them.

To reintroduce the practice of laying *tefillin* for morning prayers, Schaalman started a *Tephillin* Club. It only lasted about six months before Schaalman gave up when the attendance dropped off. Even he gave up laying *tefillin*. He recognized that to continue the practice and to wear a *kippah* and tallis meant that inevitably he was drawing attention to himself and his friends for what might be perceived by the other students as a provocation.

In fact, he was called into the president's office to answer for these actions. For Schaalman, this was an embarrassment because he revered Morgenstern and considered him his savior. Speaking to him sharply, Morgenstern said, "That as long as I was in Rome, I should do as the Romans did" (not the first time Schaalman had heard these words).[100] Morgenstern's stern rebuke reduced the young man to tears, and Schaalman concluded that Morgenstern didn't like him.

One of Morgenstern's main objections was to the recital of *birkat* prayer after meals in the dining hall. He was particularly irate that the young rabbinic student had no idea what the prayers meant. He told Schaalman, "Your version of the prayer thanks God for the good land that He has given us. You need to realize that you are in America and that this is *the good land*" [italics added].[101] He recommended that Schaalman avail himself of a *Haggadah* written by one of the faculty that excised these passages and contained an acceptable version of the *birkat hamazon*.[102]

Morgenstern called Schaalman into his office on two other occasions to read him the riot act, reminding Schaalman that he was a scholarship student and that "he should know his place." "I understood these remarks as a warning not to make waves. The memory of the encounter is still vivid to me today."[103] Without malice of forethought, Schaalman had established himself as the "bad boy" on campus!

Schaalman was not the only one of the Gang to be called into Morgenstern's office. Plaut reported that Morgenstern called him in to warn him about promoting too many of his "orthodox customs" and to tone down his support for Zionism.

Several factors could have accounted for Morgenstern's sharp reaction. He was, after all, the college president and may have thought that these refugees were testing his authority by introducing Jewish practices they knew were unacceptable. These actions would have been perceived as provocative and in need of stern rebuke, especially coming from refugees who were scholarship students and whom the college had rescued from Hitler's oppression. How audacious of them to challenge the college's administration, faculty, and student body!

Another source of Morgenstern's conflict with Schaalman and Plaut may have been the result of his very different religious upbringing. Until he was ordained in 1902, Morgenstern had never attended a Passover Seder.[104] David Komerofsky explains the, because of Morgenstern's non-observant background, "He would always feel slightly uncomfortable in traditional Jewish settings."[105] One practice that he apparently endorsed was a mealtime prayer to express thankfulness to God. At the same time, he did not accept the traditional *motzi* and *birkat hamazon* but proposed a simple English prayer in their place.

Among the HUC faculty, Morgenstern was not alone. His minimalist ritual practice was also the practice of "most of the faculty, and nearly all of the students."[106] Only a few of the HUC faculty and students kept the laws of Sabbath or of Kashrut; worship in the HUC chapel was conducted without head covering or prayer shawl. Most students came regularly to the required Shabbat services but rarely to the daily services.

STUDYING TO BE A RABBI

Bible study classes also posed a problem for the immigrant students. The Reform movement approached the Bible clinically and trained its rabbinic students accordingly. For the Gang of Five, applying critical tools to understand and interpret the Bible was a new experience. For Schaalman, the experience was totally alien. In one class, the professor told the students that for their next class they should bring an English Bible along with scissors and paste. During the class, he had them cut and paste sections of the prophetic literature in a way that allowed the text to read more naturally and logically.

This rearrangement of text using textual critical methods was meant to prove that the text had been written by different authors. This approach violated the storytelling aspect of Torah in favor of logical progression. Schaalman and his refugee colleagues thought this method a violation of the traditional texts. On the other hand, the other students, if they had qualms, didn't show them. Eventually, though, the refugee students developed a deep respect for the knowledge of some of their professors. They were very good scholars and knew not only modern scholarship but were intimately acquainted with their original sources.

Although HUC was the citadel of Reform Judaism, the movement paid little attention to theology. According to Borowitz, "Even a cursory examination of the history of the movement shows that Reform, like traditional Judaism, has been occupied mainly with the practical problems of 'living a Jewish life.'"[107] These problems included social justice, anti-Semitism, and Zionism. The movement was skeptical of theology and discussion of God, which were considered "pie in the sky."[108]

Schaalman regretted, however, that the curriculum did not include instruction in theology. What he wanted was an idea of a systematization and a coherent structure of belief. Instead, theology was taught as a separate subject and by lecture. Even if he wanted to, asking questions was not part of the learning process, not unlike his experience in German schools. In these schools, students were not given the opportunity to question, and respect for authority was a given. Schaalman, speaking for himself and possibly for his colleagues, said, "I was alone in a foreign country participating in a new religion that was totally foreign to me."[109]

A year before the German students arrived, Mordecai Kaplan had published his new book, *Judaism as a Civilization: Toward a Reconstruction of American-Jewish Life* (1934). It called for a theological reformulation of Judaism. At that time, Reform Judaism found its justification in the strict exercise of rationalist thinking. Kaplan argued that such an approach was unnecessarily limiting. He proposed that the rational understanding of Judaism had room for Judaism's "particular folk feelings and associations," which gave "full scope to man's emotive as well as his rational capacity."[110] By allowing for this emotive component, Kaplan's Judaism had more appeal to the young rabbinic students than the more austere Classical Reform.[111]

What made Kaplan's rationalism even more appealing to the rabbinic students was its American flavor. Nonetheless, he argued that a scientific methodology could be used as a way to approach theology. This methodology conflicted with supernaturalism and clashed head-on with the Jewish idea of a supernatural God, which was the basis of Reform and traditional Judaism. Kaplan's view depersonalized and demythologized God and made "Him" a process of nature. Kaplan also attacked the idea that God chose Israel, which he considered nothing more than a folk conceit. "Israel," Kaplan maintained, chose "the idea of God."[112]

Two years later, Kaplan published *Judaism in Transition* (1936), which further developed his evolving ideas. Here he argued that Judaism was in transition and would not survive with an outdated attachment to a transcendent being.[113] Such an idea no longer vitalized the Jewish people who were in search of a new view of themselves, a central core based on the reality of their condition in the modern world. Stripped of its supernaturalism and reduced to its essence, Judaism, he maintained, was first and foremost a civilization, a people. Far from advocating a pared-down Judaism, Kaplan wrote that Judaism is robust, an "organic totality" that includes all Jewish life.[114]

Because HUC students were offered little by way of theological instruction, they used their new skills in rational criticism to decide whatever theology made the most sense.[115] Some, like Schaalman, became Kaplan proselytes.

The five German refugees were excellent students. One can only imagine what it might have been like to have "bull" sessions with the likes of W. Gunther Plaut, Herman Schaalman, Alfred Wolf, Wolli Kaelter, and Leo Lichtenberg.[116] According to Schaalman, "We discussed a lot of things…simply because we felt we had a different experience, came from a different background. Yet, even though we thought that what they were learning at HUC was 'strange,' we were not opposed to it."[117] Kaelter was the only one of the five who held on to his traditional background.

It is a well-known saying that all study and no play makes a dull Jack. According to Kaelter, tennis was their game of choice. The entire student body played, especially the Germans. Plaut, who had been one of the best players on the German tennis team, gave Schaalman half a dozen lessons and even allowed him to play with him on the HUC tennis courts. From then on, tennis became one of Schaalman's lifelong passions.

Social life was another challenge. Because of his fluency in English, Plaut was socially active and a ladies' man. Unlike his German friends who didn't go out at night, Plaut frequently left the dorm for a date or for social events. One night, his friends decided to play a prank on him by changing his room number and everything else in the room. When he came back, he was completely disoriented because he had no idea where he was. Another prank involved Leo Lichtenberg, who slept a lot and very deeply. On one occasion, his friends picked him up, bed and all, and carried him into the shower.

A German refugee family named Kahn opened their home for social gatherings for German refugees, including the Gang of Five, whom they referred to as "the German boys." These social events sponsored by HUC allowed these "boys" to meet German-Jewish girls. At one of these socials, Lichtenberg met his future wife, Hilda Kahn, the daughter of the host family. The Kahns had had the good sense to leave Germany while it was still possible to get a visa to America. When they arrived in the United States, they joined an already well-established German-Jewish community in Cincinnati.

1937: Return to Germany

In 1937, Schaalman, Plaut, and Wolf returned to Germany on their round-trip tickets. By this time, most of the infamous anti-Semitic laws and government actions had been put in place. Life for Jews in Germany had become harsher and more restrictive. State governments had stopped issuing licenses to Jewish doctors, veterinarians, and pharmacists. Jews were no longer allowed to sit for professional exams, and a ban was in place to prevent anyone related by marriage to a Jew to teach in a vocational or agricultural school.[118]

The Nuremberg Laws had been enacted to protect Aryan blood, including a prohibition of marriage or sexual relations between Aryans and Jews.[119] Mixed marriages had been outlawed, as was the ability to hide one's Jewish identity by changing either one's first or last name. The schools had been racially segregated, and a German who had Jewish grandparents four generations removed was still a Jew. A German two generations removed from Jewish grandparents was one-half Jewish. These two categories, half-Jews and quarter-Jews, were not allowed to marry Aryans but only other Jews.[120]

At least four of the young men had promised their parents that they would return after two years, and each had his own reasons. Schaalman come home to attend his brother Freddie's bar mitzvah and to see his girlfriend, Lotte Strauss. He had promised her that they would get engaged when he returned. Looking back at the decision, Schaalman commented, "Returning to Germany at that time, was foolish, foolhardy... in fact, things happened then that really underscored how hare-brained it was."[121] His brother Freddie and the family thought he was "crazy" to take such a risk. Freddie couldn't understand why his father would allow his son to come home when the Nazis were putting young people who had returned from America in concentration camps. These returning young people might be spies for America.

Returning to America, however, was not a sure thing. Schaalman needed a student visa. He could have chosen to emigrate, and the Nazis would have been only too happy to see him go. However, at the time, he did not consider emigration an option. Even if he had wanted to go, given the fact that large numbers of German Jews were fleeing the country, he would have had to take his chances by subjecting himself to America's tight immigration quotas.

The only way he could get the student visa was to pull strings. His mother's cousin in Stuttgart, Oscar Wanschel, a commercial consul to the Republic of Panama, came to his rescue. Wanschel knew the American consul who had helped Herman get his first student visa. To get the visa, you had to prove that your English skills were sufficient to benefit from study in the United States. The American consul's wife, who was German, had the responsibility of certifying the young man's English skills. When Schaalman met with her over tea in her home, they spoke to each other in English: "I could barely speak," Schaalman recalled, "but she couldn't either."[122] When she reported to her husband that the young man had the requisite skills, he issued the visa.

Plaut returned to Germany because he had promised to attend his brother William's high school graduation. One of Plaut's professors had warned him not to take the chance of returning to Germany because the Nazis might not let him come back to the United States. In retrospect, Plaut characterized his decision to make this risky journey as "one of the most stupid chances I have ever taken."

In 1937, Wolf went home for a summer vacation in Eberbach. He was, however, apparently not as naive as his friends. He did some research to find out whether he would be putting himself in danger of being arrested. He turned to Officer Fleitz, who reassured him that he would be safe.

Nonetheless, when he arrived, he discovered that the police had confiscated all German passports held by Jews. Fleitz told Alfred not to worry; the passports would be returned before he had to travel to the U.S. Consulate in Stuttgart to have his immigration visa stamped into his passport. Although he was happy to have this time with his parents, he couldn't wait to go back to America, which he now considered his home. He took a train to Paris, where he planned to meet Plaut and Schaalman. They were scheduled to board a ship in Le Havre to return to America. This time, however, Alfred bought a one-way ticket. He had no plans to return to Germany. Once the train crossed the border to France, he felt the heavy burden of being in Nazi Germany lift from his shoulders: "I literally breathed more easily."[123]

Unlike his friends who waited two years to return, Kaelter had promised his parents that he would come home at the end of his first year of study. When he returned in the summer of 1936, he saw major changes in Germany brought on by the new Nuremburg Laws. Fortunately for him and his family, at this time Danzig was still "free" city and not subject to German laws. Nonetheless, the city was racked by political violence and its continuing status as a free city was uncertain. Thanks to his friend, Lou Silberman, he got an affidavit from an American citizen that would allow him to return to the U.S. as an "immigrant" and begin the process of attaining American citizenship.

During that summer of 1936, Dr. Leo Baeck secured him High Holy Days positions in Berlin. During these holidays, synagogues had more congregants than they could accommodate. Kaelter was happy to get the experience of leading a more traditional service than HUC had trained him for. Nonetheless, he never felt quite secure and worried whether he might be under surveillance by the Gestapo. When he returned to America on the Queen Mary, he was relieved that he no longer felt this threat.

Unfortunately, there is no information about whether Leo Lichtenberg returned to Germany while he was a student at HUC or at any other time.

KRISTALLNACHT

On November 9–10, 1938, Germany exploded in calculated violence against its Jews, an event that came to be known as *Kristallnacht*, the night of the broken glass.[124] SS and civilian mobs burned synagogues, trashed Jewish businesses, and beat up Jews on the streets. The police rounded up adult Jewish males, including Schaalman's and Wolf's fathers, and sent them to Dachau, a concentration camp ten miles outside of Munich. Plaut's father, Jonas, managed to escape the roundup by hiding in the home of friends. In March 1939, he and his wife escaped to America.

A new law stripped Jews of their citizenship, which meant that Jewish teachers and civil servants were forced to retire, and their children were no longer allowed to attend public schools. When Herman's brothers, Freddie and Ernst, showed up for school the next day, they were told they could no longer attend the school. Freddie dropped out, but the Schaalmans sent Ernst to a finishing school in Berlin, where he lived in a Jewish "*kinder* home." When he graduated in July 1938, they sent him to England to finish high school.

Although Adolf had been arrested during *Kristallnacht* and sent to Dachau, Regina, by pulling every political string open to her, secured his release. Up to this point, Adolf, like Jonas Plaut, had refused to leave Germany, believing he had a right to stay there. Now he realized he wasn't wanted and fled with his family to South America. Luckily, his wife's two brothers, Pinchas and Julius, who had the foresight to immigrate to South America sometime during the 1920s, helped the Schaalmans resettle there.

Schaalman and Wolf first learned about *Kristallnacht* from radio news in their dormitory. Then came the urgent telegrams from their mothers. Schaalman was assisting in conducting a wedding service for Plaut and his bride, Elizabeth Strauss, when he was called out and presented with the cable from his mother: "Father in Dachau. Save him!"

Both Wolf and Schaalman were terribly upset and tried frantically to find some way to come to their aid. Schaalman's first instinct was to appeal to people who were attending the wedding, hoping that their public stature could help him. Among the guests were Professor Englander, the officiating rabbi, and Dr. Julian Morgenstern, HUC president. As soon as the service ended, Schaalman showed the cable to Morgenstern. Morgenstern immediately made a phone call to Ohio state senator Alfred Cohen, who was also chairman of the board of the college and president of the International B'nai Brith. Cohen got in touch with the State Department, and within a few hours Schaalman was told not to worry because the roundup was a mass action and not directed at his father.

Unwilling to take any chances, Schaalman and Wolf called the Jewish ex-mayor of Cincinnati for advice and help. But their effort was in vain; there was nothing he could do. Taking matters into his own hands, Schaalman attempted to get his father out of Dachau and to bring his family to America. To do that, he needed money for transportation and a job for his father. He tried to get his father a post as a cantor or rabbi, two special categories that provided an exemption to the U.S. Immigration quota for Germans seeking refuge in America. He contacted the synagogue where he had held a student pulpit. Though the board was sympathetic, they would not offer Adolf a contract.

In the meantime, Schaalman's mother arranged for the family to immigrate to Brazil where they arrived safely in 1939. With the help of her two brothers, they reestablished themselves and developed a new line of the Schaalman family. Herman's brothers, Freddie and Ernst, developed careers, found wives, and had children.[125]

On *Kristallnacht* in Wolf's hometown of Eberbach—which had been relatively safe for Jews—storm troopers and angry mobs chanting anti-Jewish slogans attacked Jews and Jewish businesses.[126] Fleitz again came to the Wolfs' rescue. He came to their home to warn them that the Nazis were arresting all Jewish adult males and sending them to

Dachau. Although Fleitz was not able to save Alfred's father, he took Alfred's grandfather, Benjamin Levy, into "protective custody." This meant that the nearly eighty-year-old was spared the trip to Dachau but still had to spend the night in a local jail before being sent home.

As late as 1940, Wolf's parents and grandparents were among the few Jews remaining in Eberbach. On October 22 of that year, the Nazis sent them to Gurs, a concentration camp in Vichy, France.[127] Thanks to Alfred's efforts and those of Nathan Ranshoff, who Wolf wrote had "adopted him," they were released on December 3, 1941, four days before Pearl Harbor. Had they not gotten out before the United States declared war on the Axis powers, they probably would not have been given the visas. They presented their U.S. visas at the Marseilles Consulate and then left for Casablanca. From there they traveled by boat to the United States, where they arrived in early 1942. Unfortunately, Benjamin Levy did not survive the concentration camp. He died January 14, 1941. That same year, Alfred became an American citizen, which enabled his family's entry into the country.

Two days after the Nazi onslaught on the Jews of Germany, the Nazis staged a repeat performance in Danzig. Besides mass arrests and destruction of Jewish property, storm troopers razed the synagogues in Langfuhr and Zoppot. Only timely intervention by Danzig's community leaders and police, together with the aid of a group of Jewish war veterans who set up a defensive perimeter around the synagogue, saved Danzig's Great Synagogue from a similar fate. Over the course of the next few days, some fifteen hundred Jews fled over the Polish border.[128]

Kristallnacht destroyed any illusions that Jews had a future in Danzig. Its effect on the Kaelter family was catastrophic. Wolli's brother, Franz, who had already suffered the indignity of arrest by the Nazis but was later released, was forced in the middle of the night to leave his house with his wife and child, wearing only their nightclothes. While the Nazis were preparing to send Franz to a concentration camp, Wolli planned for his escape and resettlement in America. The only way Franz would be allowed to immigrate was with a special visa that was available to rabbis. By some sleight of hand, Wolli made him "a youth rabbi," but he still needed money to get Franz to Cincinnati. Wolli borrowed money from a woman who had been a member of his youth group in Germany. She came from a well-to-do family and now lived in Cincinnati. She was only too happy to help by lending the $1,500 necessary to insure Franz's salary at a local congregation. The money was put in escrow at a congregation in Indiana.

The congregation sent a telegram to the police department in Konigsberg, where Franz was being held. The telegram stated that the congregation was offering Franz a contract as a "youth rabbi." Franz was released and given two months to get out of the country. Kaelter wrote: "Although the credential was fake, the position was real." Nevertheless, Franz never did make it to America. His sister Ruth had been working on an alternative escape. She secured him an "affidavit" that would allow him entry into Palestine. Given the choice between Indiana or Palestine, he chose Palestine.[129]

In the meantime, Wolli worked "tirelessly" to get his mother to leave Danzig and come to America. For a long time, she refused. She received a state pension for her deceased husband and refused to be a financial burden on her children. The Nazis helped convince her that she'd better leave. First, they evicted her from her home and sent her to live in a building with the few Jews remaining in Danzig. Two forced Nazi transport trips to Warsaw finally convinced her. The officials took her off the train because, by then, Wolli had become an American citizen, and he could vouch for her admission to the United States. She made it out in June 1941, just before the Nazis closed off exit permits.

When she arrived in the U.S., she went straight to Cincinnati to live near Hans. According to Kaelter, she arrived "with a very guilty conscience, because she had not brought his father's rabbinic library."[130]

Although she was in her sixties, soon after she recovered her strength, she insisted that she had to support herself. She got a full-time job in the Jewish hospital in Cincinnati as a salad lady and moved out from her son's home into a rented room. By this time, Kaelter had accepted a rabbinic post in Beth Israel Synagogue in Lebanon, Pennsylvania. He had been fortunate that his mother and his siblings escaped the Nazi efforts to annihilate Polish Jews.

Unfortunately, we know next to nothing about the plight of the Lichtenberg family. All we know is that when Leo left Germany for America, he fully intended to find a sponsor to bring his mother to America. One of the great pains of his life was that he failed in getting her out in time; she perished in the Holocaust. Sadly, with one exception, his entire family died in the concentration camps.

THE STUDENTS GET MARRIED

It needs to be pointed out that all five of these rabbis married and "lived happily ever after." From their own accounts and the accounts of those who knew them, they had storybook marriages. They all married young, before they assumed their first rabbinic posts. They must have recognized that a candidate with a wife was likely to make a better impression in their efforts to land a congregation.

Wolli Kaelter was the first of the Gang to marry. While still a student at HUC, Wolli met and knew immediately he wanted to marry Sarah Shapiro, a beautiful woman six years his senior. Although not yet ordained, he bucked HUC policy and married her on July 14, 1938, two years before his ordination in 1940. It was a small wedding held at her home in Pittsburgh.

Plaut, the oldest of the five, was the next to marry. Little did he know that the date, November 10, 1938, was the turning point for German Jews and for Jews throughout Europe.[131] On *Kristallnacht*, he married Elizabeth Strauss in a small, private wedding in her home. In attendance were the other four members of the Gang, a few of Elizabeth's family, Plaut's brother, Walter, and three rabbis: Henry Englander, Dr. Julian Morgenstern, and David Philipson. Given Plaut's earlier run-in with Philipson, Plaut was not too happy to have this rabbi at his wedding. However, he had no choice: Philipson has been the Strauss family rabbi since the 1880s.

Alfred Wolf met his wife, Miriam Office, almost accidentally. While on his way home to Cincinnati from his trip to Germany in 1937, he was stranded in Dayton, Ohio. He had scheduled a ride on river boat to Cincinnati, but the Ohio River had flooded, disrupting riverboat traffic. While he was waiting for the flood to subside, he met an acquaintance from his Heidelberg days, Sigmund (Sig) Oppenheimer. Sig introduced him to Miriam Office. Not long after they started dating, the couple fell deeply in love and decided to marry after Alfred's ordination.[132] Like

Kaelter and Plaut before him, he knew that HUC frowned on ordinees marrying before their graduation, but he did it anyway. He and Miriam married on June 16, 1940.

Leo Lichtenberg continued the trend to marry before ordination. In May of 1939 he married Hilda Kahn and was ordained the next year in 1940.[133] Soon after, the Lichtenbergs left Cincinnati for Wichita Falls to take on his first rabbinic assignment.

Schaalman, the youngest of the Gang, was the last to marry. He was the only one of the Five who waited until he was ordained before he married, but not long. The afternoon of his ordination, on May 25, 1941, he married Lotte Stern. Together, they lived a full and loving life. Until he died on January 31, 2017, he would claim that he was the oldest living survivor of the Gang of Five and the oldest living Reform rabbi.

POST-GRADUATION

The hardest part of being a rabbi is remaining at the same time
a normal, warm, sensitive human being.
Rabbi Alfred Wolf ("Memories")

After their ordinations, the Gang of Five fanned out across the country. Schaalman went to Temple Judah, a small Reform congregation in Cedar Rapids. Plaut, who was two years ahead of the others, had been ordained in 1939 and took a post as assistant rabbi at Chicago's Washington Boulevard Temple.[134] Kaelter, instead of following his friends to Reform congregations, preferred a rabbinic post in a traditional congregation and found one at Beth Israel Synagogue, a tiny congregation in Lebanon, Pennsylvania. Wolf took a post at Temple Emanu-El in Dothan, Alabama, and Lichtenberg went to Temple Israel, a small Reform congregation in Wichita Falls.

Hardly had they assumed their new posts when they found that their new home country was at war with the country of their births. On December 7, 1941, the United States declared war on Japan and four days later Germany and the Axis powers. Plaut, Lichtenberg, and Schaalman wanted to volunteer to serve as chaplains in the U.S. Army but could not do so until they became citizens.[135] When Schaalman, Plaut, and Lichtenberg returned from their trip to Germany in the summer of 1937, they initiated the five-year waiting period to become citizens. In early 1943, they traveled to Cuba because they knew that if they reentered the United States from Cuba, they were eligible to apply for U.S. citizenship.

Schaalman, who did not enlist right away, was disqualified for service when, in January of 1945, he was seriously injured in an automobile accident. Plaut, on the other hand, once he received his citizenship papers on March 31, 1943, and with the approval of his congregation for a three-year leave of absence, immediately joined the United States Army. He was assigned to the 104th Infantry "Timberwolf" Division and served as a frontline chaplain in Belgium and Germany. Near the end of the war in Europe, he took part in the liberation of Germany's Dora-Nordhausen concentration camp. He also conducted the first postwar Jewish religious service in Germany's gutted Cologne Synagogue. For his meritorious service, he was awarded the Bronze Star.

Because his wife was pregnant in December 1941, Wolf never served in the military. However, he performed chaplain duties at bases across the South. To cover this large territory, he earned a pilot's license and rented single-engine planes. When he and his wife moved to Los Angeles, she made him promise he would give up his wings.

Lichtenberg, because he felt that he owed an enormous debt to the United States, almost immediately upon becoming a citizen enlisted as a chaplain in the U.S. Air Force. He wanted to be sent to Germany, but the air force sent him to Hawaii instead. When the war ended, he was put on the reserve list. In 1951, he was called up to serve in the Korean War. Fortunately for him and his family, he was posted in Biloxi, Mississippi. He retired from military service a lieutenant colonel but continued his chaplaincy as the national chaplain of the American Legion.

PART 4

Twentieth-Century Reform Judaism

WHEN THE STUDENTS ARRIVED IN America, they discovered that Judaism in America was not the Judaism they knew; to them, it was barely Judaism. The only Reform congregation in Germany that closely resembled Reform in America was in Berlin, and it used vernacular German in its prayer service.[136] In Liberal German Judaism that Schaalman was used to, women sat in a gallery or on the side of the sanctuary separate from men. According to Richter, a Liberal German synagogue had a mixed choir and organ music, but almost all the prayers were in Hebrew and followed the traditional model.[137]

At first, the students were religious outsiders. None of them knew what it meant to be a Reform Jew, much less a rabbi. At HUC, they were educated in Classical Reform Judaism, which was totally alien to them. Reform Judaism had thrown out most of traditional Judaism's liturgical practice and theology.[138] One of the first victims of this liturgical purge was *Kashrut*, the requirement to keep kosher. Another was the *kippah* and *tallit*, which were no longer allowed in Reform temples. Laying on of *tefillin* also was abandoned; prayer services were shortened and, because most Reform Jews could not read Hebrew, they were conducted in English. Now, women and men could sit together in the service.

Congregations could reschedule Shabbat services if Saturday morning was inconvenient for their members. Sermons could be anything the rabbi thought might interest his congregation. Books and politics were frequent choices.[139]

Although the Gang of Five didn't know it at the time, Reform Judaism was then, as it is today, in a continuous state of change. In 1937, two years after they arrived at HUC, the Central Conference of American Rabbis (CCAR) issued a new declaration of principles known as the Columbus Platform. It was a radical departure from its Pittsburgh Platform (1885), Reform Judaism's founding declaration of principles. In that first document, God was referred to as the "God-idea." The wording effectively neutered the reality of an existing God. The 1937 Platform stated unequivocally that:

> God was at the heart of Judaism and its chief contribution to religion is the doctrine of the One, living God, who rules the world through law and love. In Him all existence has its creative source and mankind its ideal of conduct. Though transcending time and space, He is the indwelling Presence of the world. We worship Him as the Lord of the universe and as our merciful Father.[140]

The 1937 Platform also placed a new emphasis on tradition and the importance of holding on to rituals and beliefs that the early reformers had abandoned. Since then, Reform has continued to move in the direction of restoring more traditional ritual and belief.[141]

For the Gang of Five, change was not easy. As students at HUC, they had to undergo a difficult transition from their more traditional European cultural and religious backgrounds to become rabbis trained in Classical Reform. How did they react to the changes occurring in Reform Judaism over the next few decades? The record is clear for

Schaalman and Plaut, but none of the others left any indication of their response to these changes, and whatever divergent views they may have had, they chose not to make their views public.[142] Schaalman and Plaut, however, were not content with the changes in Reform and were outspoken critics.

Schaalman claimed that he and his refugee colleagues had no intention of overthrowing or rebelling against Reform Judaism. Nevertheless, their attempt to introduce traditional liturgical practices in the seminary was the first sign of the impact they would have on Reform Judaism in the twentieth century.[143] At the same time, they too were radically transformed by their training as Reform rabbis, a transformation that allowed them to become part of the Reform establishment, as well as agents of change.[144]

REFORM JEWISH CAMPING

One of the most important changes for Reform Judaism coming on the heels of WWII was the sense that the future of Judaism depended on educating its youth. This reaction was a response to the slaughter of six million Jews, one million of them children.[145] Jacob Sarna writes that there was a growing sense in the American Jewish community that it was taking on a new, historic role: to protect and perpetuate the Jewish heritage, its culture, and civilization. The cultural transfer from Europe to America meant that going forward, America was now the repository of that culture.[146]

This transfer had a direct impact on the development of Jewish camping in America. Many of the refugees had benefited from Zionist youth experiences in Germany and other parts of Europe. In their adopted country, they considered that these experiences were fundamental in their development as Jews and Zionists. Schaalman, Kaelter, and Wolf, who had all been participants in Jewish youth movements in Germany, played a major role in propelling this movement forward.[147]

Even before World War II, the organized body of Reform Judaism, the Union of American Hebrew Congregations (UAHC) had recognized the potential of such camps and set aside funds as seed money.[148] In 1943, UAHC's newly appointed president, Maurice Eisendrath, made establishing youth camps one of his priorities. But because a war was on, he was forced to put this goal on the back burner. At the UAHC biennial in 1946, however, he used his State of the Union address to advocate for an expanded youth program, including the establishment of a summer youth camp, which could also be used year-round for institutes for adult retreats and teachers.[149] He believed these summer camps would provide Reform youth an experience through which they could grow and develop a deeper understanding of and commitment to Reform Judaism. He also believed in the merits of three members of the Gang of Five. He hired them as UAHC outreach liaisons: Schaalman in the Midwest,

Wolf in Southern California, and Kaelter in Northern California, and gave them the responsibility for developing the first UAHC-sponsored camps.

By 1950, the UAHC was ready to move forward in establishing summer camps. As the Midwest director of the UAHC, Schaalman took the lead in establishing the first of these camps, the Union Institute in Oconomowoc, Wisconsin. From the beginning of the Reform Jewish camping experience, and as the prototype for the development of a network of UAHC camps in other parts of the country, the Union Institute (subsequently renamed Olin Sang Ruby Union Institute, OSRUI) "became a programmatic and liturgical crucible ever enhancing and advancing Jewish expression in the Reform movement."[150] According to Richter, OSRUI was responsible for bringing forth "so many young leaders and stands as a monument to [Schaalman's] courage and wisdom."[151]

Two others followed quickly in California: Camp Hess Kramer (1952) under the direction of Alfred Wolf, and Camp Saratoga (later named Camp Swig) under the direction of Wolli Kaelter.[152] In the summer of 1952 when Schaalman and his wife, Lotte, were setting up the first UAHC camp in Oconomowoc, Wisconsin, he asked Kaelter and his wife, Sarah, to join them. Kaelter was only too happy to oblige. In return for his help, Schaalman recommended Kaelter to Eisendrath for camp director on the West Coast. The UAHC had purchased a camp in Saratoga, California, and was seeking someone to get it up and running. Although Kaelter had no experience of this kind (neither did Schaalman or Wolf), he accepted Eisendrath's offer, which was sweetened by the assignment of directorship of the UAHC Northern California region.

On his way from McKeesport, Pennsylvania, where he led a small congregation, Kaelter stopped off to seek Wolf's advice on how to set up a camp. Wolf had already started Wilshire Boulevard's Camp Hess Kramer (1952). Kaelter wrote, "While I was very familiar with programming, I had no idea about dieticians, menus, purchasing, or maintenance."

Wolf helped establish other camps in California. For his contribution, his Wilshire Boulevard Temple memorialized him by naming an overlook along Pacific Coast Highway near Camp Hess Kramer as "Rabbi Alfred Wolf Inspiration Point." In 1955, the temple also placed a huge menorah on top of it, a testament to Rabbi Wolf's leadership and his role in establishing the camp. Subsequently his congregation named a seven-hundred-seat stone amphitheater at Hess Kramer and a smaller amphitheater at Hilltop in his honor.[153]

As the camps proliferated in the 1950s, "a whole generation of young, impressionable American Jews came under [their] spell...some young people were 'molded by them,' others 'transformed'—and from their ranks the next generation of rabbis, scholars, and lay leaders emerged."[154] These educational camps "became the cornerstone in the future structure of American Jewish education," all because of the efforts of three of the Gang of Five.[155]

REFORM'S THEOLOGICAL UNREST

While UAHC began creating summer camps for Reform Jewish youth, a hunger for theological discussion was growing among younger rabbis across the religious spectrum. From the time Schaalman was a rabbinic student at HUC, he had been unhappy with Reform's apparent lack of interest in theology and spiritual experience. What he didn't know at the time was that Classical Reform's ethical humanism was giving way to a more traditional faith-based Judaism, which Michael Meyer called in his history of Reform Judaism, *Response to Modernity*, an about-face for Reform theology.[156]

As these new currents were bubbling up in the late '40s, the CCAR decided to act. In 1950, it organized the Institute on Reform Jewish

Theology to address theological issues that had been overshadowing Reform in the first half of the twentieth century. The Institute reflected the fact that rabbis like Schaalman and Plaut were undergoing profound theological struggles that lay just beneath the surface of Judaism and Reform Judaism in particular. Attended by only a handful of rabbis, the Institute failed to accomplish its objective of developing a consensus for a new direction for Reform Judaism.

The issue, however, was not dead. Six years later, Schaalman and his friend from his student years at HUC, Lou Silberman, initiated a series of conferences with the ambitious goal of creating "a new theology for Reform Judaism."[157] Held initially at the Union Institute, the conferences gave Schaalman and Plaut the opportunity to meet with other young rabbis and scholars who were soon to become some of the most influential Jewish thinkers in America.[158] These participants rejected earlier Reform theology, which they considered superficial because it had sidelined God and thus lost its spiritual center. In their effort to rediscover Judaism's roots, these rabbis found them in the irrevocable covenant that God had established with Israel.

COVENANTAL THEOLOGY

The young rabbis who attended these conferences proved to be in the vanguard of ideas that were radically reshaping Liberal Judaism. In 1969, Borowitz labeled this new direction "Covenantal Theology."[159] The main tenets of this group were that: through the covenant, God and the people Israel, God and the individual Jew, are bound in an eternal bond of mutual responsibilities; this relationship is dynamic and fundamentally two-way. For Reform Judaism, this relationship meant that humans whom God had endowed with freedom, autonomy, and the ability to think for themselves, were responsible and obligated to decide what parts of the "received tradition" were relevant to their contemporary experience.[160] It is a perspective that Schaalman adopted wholeheartedly.

The prime movers in this new development—Fackenheim, Borowitz, and Plaut—were Schaalman's friends and colleagues. As Covenantal Theologians, they could resist the temptation to allow the events of the *Shoah* to overwhelm them. Despite the fact of God's apparent absence, they put their trust in the belief that He would fulfill His part of the covenant by His eventual presence.[161]

In 1965, Plaut identified another development in Reform, which he called an emerging "pietistic" wing.[162] This "wing," he wrote, was less interested in maintaining the distinction of Reform from traditional Judaism than in moving Reform closer to embracing in both spirit and practice *Klal Yisrael* (the idea of the inclusiveness of the Jewish people).[163]

Although Plaut did not take ownership of this trend, he was sympathetic, a fellow traveler, if you will. From his earliest years at HUC, he had been uncomfortable with Classical Reform because of its near-total divorce from tradition. He rejected the notion that Reform Jews had complete autonomy to accept or reject whatever aspects of Judaism they thought appropriate. In his *The Case for the Chosen People*, he argued that "Judaism without all authority was an oxymoron."[164] In the 1960s, battle lines had formed between rabbis who wanted total autonomy and those who, like Plaut, wanted more authority.[165]

In the 1970s, Reform took on two of its most controversial issues, mixed marriage and patrilineal descent. Both issues had to do with inclusion. A significant portion of the Reform rabbinate, concerned about declining synagogue membership and more socially liberal than their predecessors, wanted to open Reform to interfaith families. Schaalman and Plaut were unhappy with this direction. Both had undergone a difficult transition from their more conservative German cultural and religious backgrounds and were now resistant to many of the proposed changes. They now represented the "old guard," and as the older generation of Reform rabbis, they were now resistant to many of the proposed changes. When both became presidents of the CCAR in the 1980s, they were outspoken critics of the proposed changes to rabbinic officiation at mixed marriages and to the traditional principle of matrilineal descent.

While Schaalman rose in prestige and influence within the Reform movement, it was moving to address the issues of its restive congregations. In 1975, the CCAR issued *Gates of Prayer* (GOP) to replace *The Union Prayer Book*, Reform's first prayer book, which was now considered outmoded. Included in the GOP was the use of contemporary English; an unprecedented selection of new prayers, readings, and meditations to accompany the Hebrew text; and services for Holocaust commemoration and Israeli Independence Day. For Schaalman, although the prayer book was an improvement, it still included the old hierarchical language based on God as King and the theology it represented. He wanted a prayer service that captured some of the mystery and excitement of the Jewish experience, particularly the experience of the Revelation at Sinai.

In addition to the CCAR's attempt to modernize the prayer book, the decision also represented a turn toward tradition. According to D. E. Kaplan, Reform Jews were seeking more security in tradition and, although these changes were, in a sense, anachronistic, they appear to have been a response to the needs of the majority of contemporary Reform congregants. Their goal "[was] to situate themselves within a historical religion that allows them to explore a range of spiritual paths not limited to artificial boundaries."[166]

Despite his traditionalist bent, Plaut played a major role in the effort to "modernize" Reform Judaism. Urged on by key leaders in the movement, he took on the job of writing a series of books that provided the intellectual and scholarly base for the changes that he thought desirable.[167] The job also was an opportunity for him to assert his more traditional views. The books included *The Case for the Chosen People* (1965); *Genesis: A Commentary* (1974), and his masterpiece, *The Torah: A Modern Commentary* (1981). Plaut's efforts to assert traditional precedent, however, got him in deep trouble with his colleagues and cost him the CCAR presidency. He was ahead of his time.

COMMITTEE ON MIXED MARRIAGE

Other forces for change were at work during this period. The 1960s were a time of great social upheaval. Freedom was in the air and demands for change in established beliefs and practices were the prevailing cultural mantra. Jewish youths played a major role in this movement. They struck out into a variety of liberal causes, including new freedoms of self-expression and the longstanding issues of segregation, poverty, and social justice. On the heels of this new freedom, many of them were intermarrying. These new developments reflected the fact that younger Jews were not as strongly attached to Judaism as were their parents. While the number of interfaith marriages among Jews was increasing, the ranks of the American Jewish population were declining. Jewish leaders were convinced that the survival of Judaism in America was at stake and rushed to find ways to stem the rising tide of disaffection.

Members of the Reform rabbinate were no less affected. In the late '60s, a small group of them pushed the CCAR to recognize that a significant number of rabbis were performing mixed marriages and that the policy against this practice needed to change. During the first sixty years of the twentieth century, CCAR had tried to combat this practice by passing resolutions prohibiting it, but the effort failed. The number of rabbis performing mixed marriages was growing.[168] They argued that refusing to officiate at these weddings would further alienate the Jewish spouse, whose attachment to Judaism was already tenuous. Inclusion, they insisted, was better for the survival of the Jewish people than exclusion.[169]

The CCAR knew it had to act, if only to counter this growing threat. In 1971, it resurrected a standing but moribund Committee on Mixed Marriage and turned to Schaalman to provide leadership to address the issue. Suddenly he was thrust into the limelight. Before then, he had no official role in CCAR, though he was well respected by his colleagues. One of the factors that led to his appointment as chair of the committee was that in the same year, he had written a paper for CCAR arguing that officiation in interfaith marriages would drive a wedge between liberal and traditional segments of Judaism: "Whatever endangers the survival of the Jewish people…whatever fragments it further is intolerable today. Our officiating at marriages between Jews and non-Jews is a divisive element widening the gap irretrievably between the torn fragments of our people."[170]

Another factor that weighed heavily in the decision to appoint him was the fact that Schaalman did not have Plaut's reputation as an outspoken right-winger with a strong tendency toward Orthodoxy. His attempt to push Reform toward more traditional practice earned him this reputation among more liberal rabbis. Schaalman got the assignment because he was well respected by his colleagues for his evenhandedness, his calm demeanor, and his temperament. Moreover, unlike Plaut, he had not staked out a theological position. The CCAR leadership saw him as a representative of the old guard who could be counted on to channel the discussion of this contentious issue toward CCAR's longstanding position against rabbinic officiation at mixed (interfaith) marriages.[171]

After two years of contentious deliberations, the committee produced a hard-won compromise recommendation that "rabbis refrain" from officiating at mixed marriages. However, as the result of a floor fight at the CCAR's 1973 Annual Convention, the committee's recommendation was amended to read: "The Central Conference of American Rabbis recognizes that historically its members have held and continue to hold divergent interpretations of Jewish tradition."[172] For the organization's leadership, and for Schaalman personally, this development was a major defeat.

COMMITTEE ON PATRILINEAL DESCENT

Over the next six years, a related issue surfaced and demanded attention: patrilineal descent. Traditionally, the offspring of a Jewish marriage were automatically Jewish if the mother was Jewish. Why couldn't and why shouldn't that right also be extended to the father? Equality of the sexes went hand in hand with equality of females. The feminist movement had thrown open the doors to the question, why should only mothers determine the Jewishness of a child? Why not fathers as well?

The need to address this problem was reaching critical proportions. According to Jewish demographic data, the number of Americans who identified as Jews was declining.[173] All three branches of Judaism were worried about how to reverse this trend. For Reform Judaism, the increasing number of interfaith marriages meant that the offspring of these marriages were at risk of being raised as gentiles. By 1980, Jewish population growth had stagnated.[174] Part of the reason was the aging of the population, postponement of marriage, low fertility, more frequent intermarriage, and "the nonattribution of Jewish identification to high percentages of the children of one non-Jewish parent."[175] The handwriting was on the wall, and the CCAR realized it had act to address what it thought was shaping up as a dire situation.

In 1979, the CCAR established a new committee, the Blue Ribbon Committee on Patrilineal Descent, and appointed Schaalman as its chair. That same year, the CCAR had appointed him as its vice president, a stepping stone to his becoming president in 1981. He now had a dual leadership role, but the CCAR leadership assumed the committee's work would be done before he became president, so that there would be no conflict of interest. It is a testament to Schaalman's standing in the organization that his colleagues would put him in two positions of such great responsibility. By rights, the vice president position should have gone to Plaut. Having been ordained two years before Schaalman, Plaut was his senior. The honor went to Schaalman because Plaut's strident advocacy had made him a controversial figure and, as he wrote in *Unfinished Business*, too conservative.[176] Schaalman was now in a position to play a pivotal role in Reform's effort to modernize itself.

The issue of patrilineal descent proved to be even more contentious and intractable than the issue of mixed marriage. The committee's deliberations lingered on into Schaalman's presidency. As chair of the Committee on Patrilineal Descent and the CCAR's president, he presented the committee's resolution at the CCAR's Annual Convention in 1981, where it ran into a firestorm of debate.

The controversial resolution was attacked from the floor, some of the strongest objections coming from Plaut, who had been a member of the committee. He did not see any reason to change what was then current Reform rabbinic practice. Reform rabbis, he argued, already had the latitude to make their own decisions about how to deal with interfaith families. Many of them allowed children with a Jewish father but a non-Jewish mother to become Jews, as long as the parents committed to raising their children as Jews, including attending Hebrew school, participating in religious services, and becoming a bar or bat mitzvah. New policies, he argued vehemently, must be based on precedent in Jewish law, and there was no precedent for patrilineal descent: "Simply overriding two millennia of Jewish history was the wrong way to approach the problem." He went on to argue that to change that practice into a ruling was a huge mistake. It would redefine who was a Jew and exacerbate the growing divide between Reform and Orthodox Judaism.

Plaut put forward what he thought was a decent compromise, namely that a child born of a Jewish father and a non-Jewish mother would be presumed "half Jewish" and could then be presumed to be on a course to become Jewish through the normal conversion process. After hours of deliberation, the original motion was amended and sent back to committee. Two more years passed before the CCAR heard the committee's revised resolution.

When the committee reintroduced its resolution at the 1983 Annual Conference, it continued to provoke passionate debate. Nevertheless, in a radical departure from tradition, the Reform rabbis overturned Jewish law and traditional practice by affirming that if certain conditions were met (namely that the parents promised to raise their children as Jews), the offspring of a mixed marriage in which only one partner was Jewish, *either* the father or the mother, could be considered Jewish.[177] The resolution stated:

> Depending on circumstances, mitzvot leading toward a positive and exclusive Jewish identity will include entry into the covenant, acquisition of a Hebrew name, Torah study, Bar/Bat Mitzvah, and Kabbalat Torah (Confirmation). For those beyond childhood claiming Jewish identity, other public acts or declarations may be added or substituted after consultation with their rabbi.[178]

Plaut lost what he considered a major argument that would have protected Reform from falling afoul of traditional Judaism. In hindsight, he acknowledged that his CCAR colleagues' decision was based in part on the fact that they were unwilling to allow their Orthodox colleagues, who didn't accept them anyway, to dictate what Reform could do.[179] He knew that traditional Judaism would exact its revenge—and, of course, it did. Orthodox rabbis, particularly those in Israel who were already unsympathetic to Reform, now announced that they no longer considered Reform a legitimate branch of Judaism and would no longer recognize its conversions, marriages, and its members' Right of Return to Israel as Jews. Reform Jews would have to undergo an Orthodox conversion to be considered legitimate Jews.[180]

According to Folb, "With mixed marriage, there were grey areas where remedies were possible...The CCAR position on patrilineality created an irreversible condition."[181] Richard G. Hirsch, president of the World Union of Progressive Judaism, commented, "Everybody in the World movement was opposed to it."[182]

The two conferences in 1981 and 1983 proved to be a test of Schaalman's ability to lead Reform Judaism. During his tenure, he managed to steer the CCAR through two of its most contentious issues in the face of a passionately divided rabbinate.

With the decisions on mixed marriage and patrilineal descent, Reform was venturing into unchartered territory, which both Schaalman and Plaut opposed. Nevertheless, as CCAR presidents, they were compelled to defend the organization's new policies against the objections of their Conservative and Orthodox colleagues. For Plaut, one of his most difficult tasks was to explain the policy on patrilineality to his Canadian colleagues, who were mostly opposed.

On the issue of Reform embracing more traditional practice and belief, Schaalman had strong reservations, which he made known as part of his 1981 presidential address.[183] If there were to be changes, he argued, they needed to result from formal discussion of theological issues within the CCAR.[184] It is ironic that the turn toward traditional practices were the same that he and the Gang tried, without success, to introduce when they were students at HUC. Now that he was part of the old guard of what formerly had been for him an alien Judaism, he fought to protect it.

PART 5

Contributions of the Gang of Five to Reform Judaism

———

LICHTENBERG

As INDIVIDUAL RABBIS, WOLF, KAELTER, Schaalman, and Plaut, four of the five members of the Gang of Five, made important contributions to the reform of Reform Judaism. Unfortunately, because Lichtenberg left neither an autobiographical record nor a scholarly record, his contributions are more difficult to assess. Karl Richter, however, includes him as one of the five who helped transform modern Reform Judaism.

Although Lichtenberg held pulpits in Wichita Falls, Texas, and Charlottesville, Virginia, his major work was as a Hillel Foundation director at several universities: University of Virginia, Ohio University, Hofstra University (1954–1968) and Adelphi University (1954–1968). In December 1965, he was elected president of the National Association of Hillel Directors.[185] He is credited for his introduction of Judaic Studies at Adelphi.[186] He was also a member of the executive committee of the CCAR.[187]

Unlike the other members of the Gang of Five, Lichtenberg wasn't out to change Reform Judaism or to establish new camps for Jewish youth. His daughter, Ruth Levor, describes him as a "humble" man who lived modestly and chose to devote his life to helping young people, particularly college students. He spent most of his rabbinic life as a Hillel director. As a pulpit rabbi, he acted in an assisting role, such as backup for rabbis in the communities where he lived and ritual leader in towns where there was no formal Jewish community. When the family lived in Athens, Ohio, a small Midwestern town with only a handful of Jews, Lichtenberg held services in his living room.

His humility, however, did not prevent him from taking strong advocacy positions on matters of principle. One of his primary concerns was the survival of Judaism, which he understood to mean that Judaism should never close its doors to people who might be influenced to become Jews. In this regard, although he did not advocate changes in CCAR practice, he was an early advocate of rabbinic officiation in interfaith marriages at a time when it was not popular among his Reform colleagues. He understood that many younger Jews were intermarrying, and he did not want them or their spouses to feel excluded from being part of the Jewish people.[188] Levor remembers, "Many a young couple appeared at our front door and were welcomed into dad's study for a conversation about their motivations and their plans." Her father was willing to marry them provided they agreed to his liberal terms. Some, he married in his living room. Levor reports her father saying, "Why lose one, when I may gain two?"[189] Many of the young couples whom he married returned to him for instruction and ultimately conversion.

KAELTER

Kaelter's major contribution to Reform Judaism came in his spearheading the development of the West Coast youth summer camps with the support of the UAHC director, Maurice Eisendrath. Kaelter's decision to accept this position proved to be a turning point in his career as a rabbi. This professional journey led him to a rabbinic post at Temple Israel of Long Beach, California. There he was known for his innovations in worship service and his creative programming. As with all the members of the Gang of Five, he believed strongly in interfaith outreach and devoted a substantial part of his lifetime work to interfaith activities. For twenty-five years, he taught practical rabbinics at the Hebrew Union College-Jewish Institute of Religion in Los Angeles. In this capacity, he had a major influence in guiding rabbinic students toward their rabbinates in the twenty-first century.

In 1995, the LA branch of Hebrew Union College held a sixtieth anniversary to celebrate both Kaelter's and Wolf's arrival in America. About the event, Kaelter wrote in his autobiography that he was surprised that the approximately fifty rabbis who attended the event referred to him as "a beloved elder statesman." He was embarrassed at suddenly becoming a 'historical' figure. He thought of himself at best as "respected but not necessarily loved…. I preferred to say what I thought and, if that turned out to be contentious, so be it."[190]

WOLF

Rabbi Samson H. Levey wrote that Alfred Wolf's contributions encompassed "every phase and function of the American synagogue."[191] From his relatively humble beginnings as a newly minted rabbi at Temple Emanu-El in Dothan, Alabama, Wolf became a leading figure in West Coast Reform Judaism. Among Wolf's accomplishments was his work in helping to launch the Los Angeles College of Jewish Studies for the training of religious schoolteachers for children and teachers of adults. A few years later, in the early 1950s, the college became the first Los Angeles campus of the Hebrew Union College. Later, he was asked by the renowned Rabbi Edgar F. Magnin and Rabbi Maxwell Dubin to join them as the third rabbi of Wilshire Boulevard Temple, the largest Reform congregation in the West and one of the most prominent in the world. When Magnin died in 1984, Wolf, who had already been performing the duties of the senior rabbi, took on the role before retiring the following year.

From 1946 to 1949, while he served as the UAHC West Coast director, he started eighteen Reform congregations throughout the West Coast to accommodate the postwar influx of Jews to the West. In 1952, he founded Camp Hess Kramer and Gindling Hilltop Camp in Malibu. He was the founding president of the Inter-Religious Council of Southern California. At a time when "interreligious" meant Christians and Jews, he made a point of including every major faith group, Muslims, Sikhs, Buddhists, and Hindus. Together, they tackled real issues such as abortion and Israel, finding areas of agreement and areas where they would agree to disagree.

His leadership on interfaith matters was very much prompted by his experience in Germany, where he felt Hitler rose to power because different communities didn't know each other.[192] Most noteworthy: at his funeral, two of the speakers were a Catholic monsignor and a Muslim leader. The interdenominational nature of the clerical presence was apparent in the vivid assortment of religious dress.[193] In 1987, when Pope John Paul II was visiting LA, the Pope held a historic interfaith gathering at which there were four speakers—Muslim, Hindu, Buddhist and, representing LA's Jews, Alfred Wolf.

After becoming rabbi emeritus with the Wilshire Temple, Wolf became executive director of the Skirball Institute on American Values. His motivation can be traced back to his gratitude to the country he felt saved his life and gave him the ability to lead the life of his choosing.

Wolf also was an accomplished academic. In 1960, he earned his PhD in comparative religions at the University of Southern California. Three years prior, he and Joseph Gaer published *Our Jewish Heritage* (New York: Holt, Second Edition 1958), a significant contribution to American Jewish literature.

SCHAALMAN

Schaalman's appointment as chair of the Committee on Mixed Marriage was the beginning of his unanticipated and unplanned ascent into the leadership of the CCAR, Reform's largest professional rabbinic organization with an international membership. For almost two decades, Schaalman held several of its most important positions: Chair of the Committee on Mixed Marriage (1971-1973); Chair of the Committee on Patrilineal Descent (1989-1983); CCAR Vice President (1979-1982). CCAR President (1982-1983). At the end of his term as president, Schaalman was appointed to chair the Ethics Committee, a position he held until 1989.

After his retirement as Emanuel's senior rabbi in 1986, Schaalman was free to pursue his long-term interest in promoting interfaith understanding and tolerance. Together with several of Chicago's chief clerics, he founded and became the first president of the Council of Religious Leaders of Metropolitan Chicago. Working together with these clerics, he represented Chicago's Jewish community in the successful and highly regarded organization. His partnership in this enterprise with Chicago's famed archbishop, Cardinal Joseph Bernardin, created a deep friendship between the two men. The friendship was so strong that when Bernardin was near death, he asked Schaalman to participate as one of the officiants at his funeral. That participation was the first time a rabbi had ever spoken at the funeral of a Catholic priest.

PLAUT

Plaut is by far the most accomplished of the Gang of Five, and it is fitting that we end this discussion of the Gang of Five with a brief survey of his extraordinary contributions to Reform Judaism, to Judaism in general, and to the secular world. After the war, he held pulpits in Chicago and St. Paul, Michigan, before taking up his last post in Toronto's famed Holy Blossom Temple. A past president of the CCAR and the Canadian Jewish Congress, he was named an Officer of the Order of Canada.[194]

Beginning in 1961, in a stunning display of academic scholarship and in the short span of five years, Plaut published five major books: *The Book of Proverbs—A Commentary*; *Judaism and the Scientific Spirit*; *The Rise of Reform Judaism*; *The Growth of Reform Judaism*; and *The Case for the Chosen People*. An additional book, *Your Neighbor is a Jew*, along with a stream of articles on contemporary secular issues in various periodicals, capped an astonishingly creative period of contributions to Jewish rabbinic and intellectual life. Ron Csillag wrote, "He took on all the epic battles of the day: the fight to free Soviet Jews, neo-Nazis in Canada, and large-scale rallies and political persuasion to support Israel."[195] He made his voice heard as a prolific columnist for the Canadian newspapers, the *Globe and Mail* and the *Toronto Star*. His column in the *Globe* became a regular feature throughout the '70s and '80s.

Although Plaut was disappointed that the CCAR chose Schaalman over him as its president, he eventually got the recognition he deserved.[196] This disappointment, however, allowed him to channel his energy into religious writings, including *Shaarei Mitzvah*,[197] and *Shabbat Manual*, which he edited.[198] In 1981, he published his autobiography, *Unfinished Business*, and his magnum opus, *The Torah: A Modern Commentary*, a work that took seventeen years to complete. It was the first Torah commentary in English since the publication of the Hertz *Pentateuch and Haftorahs*, issued in the late 1920s and '30s.

The Torah: A Modern Commentary received universal acclaim and established him as the preeminent scholar of Reform Judaism. It demonstrated definitively that Reform took scholarship and tradition seriously and helped establish Reform Judaism as a legitimate branch of Judaism. Reform congregations around the country and worldwide adopted the book. Robert Alter, an authority on biblical scholarship and a translator and commentator on the Torah, wrote, "With the publication of this volume, American Reform Judaism has come fully of age."[199] According to David J. Zucker, the *Commentary* was the first liberal Torah commentary ever published: "For the world of Progressive Judaism, it became the standard Torah commentary for synagogues. It was as important a volume as the monumental Hertz *Pentateuch and Haftorahs* was for the English-speaking Jewish world when published back in the 1930s."[200]

Not willing to let matters rest with this accomplishment, Plaut set out to produce a Haftorah commentary of similar importance. In 1996, he published the *Haftorah Commentary,* a capstone to Plaut's remarkable and brilliant career as a biblical scholar.

By 2005, Plaut knew he had developed Alzheimer's disease. After a seven-year battle, he died in 2012 at the remarkable age of ninety-nine. At his death, Margalit Fox of the *New York Times* wrote that Plaut's "vast, scholarly and ardently contemporary edition of the Torah has helped define Reform Judaism in late-twentieth-century North America."[201] Fox might have added that as president of CCAR and through his enormous influence in Reform Judaism, Plaut was a strong advocate for a conservative approach to the reforms of Reform during his active rabbinate.

In 1982, Robert Gordis had already written that Plaut, as a German refugee, brought "all the values of the German-Jewish community…to creative tension with the pragmatic spirit of North American Judaism.… The age-old dichotomy of tradition versus modernity he has resolved by stressing the values of tradition for modernists."[202] It is perhaps ironic that his emphasis on a Reform Judaism anchored in tradition became the basis for CCAR's new Pittsburg platform issued in 1999. Yet, from the time of the Gang's arrival in the United States, Reform has turned toward a more traditional Judaism that the early reformers had rejected.

PART 6

Conclusion

———

THE CONTRIBUTIONS OF THE GANG of Five helped write the history of twentieth-century Reform Judaism. Karl Richter wrote: "Over the years, Leo Lichtenberg, Wolli Kaelter, Herman Schaalman, W. Gunther Plaut, and Alfred Wolf would have a remarkable impact, attaining prominence as rabbis, scholars, and community leaders."[203] But as German refugee rabbis, they were not alone. In the last two decades of the twentieth century, all the leadership positions in Reform's major organizations were filled by refugee rabbis from Nazi Germany: Rabbis Alexander Schindler, head of the Union of Reform Judaism (formerly the UAHC); Schaalman and Plaut, presidents of the CCAR; and Alfred Gottschalk, president HUC-JIR.[204] Add to that mix two other German-Jewish refugees from Nazi Germany, philosopher Emil Fackenheim and Rabbi Leo Baeck, and you have a powerhouse of German Jews helping to reshape Reform Judaism of their time. Reform would not be what it is today without their exceptional leadership, character, intelligence, and energy.

ENDNOTES

---

1   Richard Damashek, *A Brand Plucked from the Fire: The Life of Rabbi Herman E. Schaalman* (Jersey City, NJ: KTAV Publishing House, Inc., 2013), 56. "Schaalman and Wolf were the youngest of the five, Lichtenberg and Kaelter were one year ahead of them, and W. Gunther Plaut was their senior by two years."

2   The seminary had been known as the *Hochschule für die Wissenschaft des Judentums*, until 1934 when the Nazis downgraded it to the less-prestigious *Lehranstalt für die Wissenschaft des Judentums*, a technical school or institute.

3   Remarkably, except for Lichtenberg who died August 5, 1977, at the age of 62, the others lived comparatively long lives: Alfred Wolf died on August 1, 2004, at the age of eighty-eight; Wolli Kaelter, on January 10, 2008, at the age of ninety-four; Gunther Plaut on February 8, 2012, at the age of ninety-nine after a long illness; Herman Schaalman, the last of the Five, on January 31, 2017, at the age of one hundred. Until his death, Schaalman claimed that he was the oldest living survivor of the Gang of Five and the oldest living Reform rabbi.

4   When Hebrew Union College merged with the Jewish Institute of
     Religion in 1950, it became Hebrew Union College-Jewish Institute
     of Religion (HUC-JIR). When reference is made to the seminary
     after 1950, it will be referred to as HUC-JIR.

5   Michael M. Lorge and Gary P. Zola, "The Beginnings of Union
     Institute in Oconomowoc, Wisconsin," in *A Place of Our Own*,
     ed. Michael M. Lorge and Gary P. Zola (Tuscaloosa: University
     of Alabama Press, 2006), 57. Lorge and Zola prefer to identify the
     seminary as *Hochschule für die Wissenschaft des Judentums*, although
     they acknowledge the change in the name to *Lehranstalt für die
     Wissenschaft des Judentums*. The name of the institution depends on
     the choice of different writers. See Michael A. Meyer in *Response to
     Modernity* (New York: Oxford University Press, 1988), 205; Wolli
     Kaelter and Gordon Cohn, *From Danzig: An American Rabbi's
     Journey* (Malibu, CA: Pangloss Press, 1997), 6; and Damashek, *A
     Brand*, 50.

6   Ann Folb, *An Intellectual and Historical Biography of Rabbi Herman
     Schaalman*, Unpublished master's thesis. (Cincinnati, OH: Hebrew
     Union College-Jewish Institute of Religion, 2007), 21.

7   Ibid., 31.

8   From 1935 to 1942, HUC rescued eleven Jewish scholars from
     Nazi persecution and revived the careers for some who had al-
     ready left Germany. HUC also saved the lives of a few others.
     Meyer claims that the "number of refugees from the Liberal
     Seminary in Berlin...made up 12 percent" of HUC's student
     body. See Michael A. Meyer, "The Refugee Scholars Project of
     the Hebrew Union College," in Bertram Wallace Korn, ed. *A

Bicentennial Festschrift for Jacob Rader Marcus (New York: KTAV, 1976), 312, 359–375.

9   Kaelter, *From Danzig*, 44.

10   Ibid.

11   Gunther Plaut, *Unfinished Business: An Autobiography* (Toronto: Lester & Orpen Dennys, Ltd., 1981), 47.

12   Ibid.

13   Kaelter, *From Danzig*, 44.

14   Alfred Wolf, "Collected Memories of Rabbi Alfred Wolf, aka Dad, aka Papa," (unpublished manuscript, 1986), #385, 172. The format for all subsequent references to the "Collected Memories" will be presented as "Memories," section #, page.

15   Damashek, *A Brand*, 52.

16   Ibid., 53. Dan Wolf, Rabbi Wolf's son, wrote, "My father's account was that he and Schneemann (I assume it was him) were the two most junior applicants and, for this reason, it came down to the two of them drawing straws to determine which would go, but Schneemann then chose not to go. My understanding is that this was because he heard from his parents that they did not favor his departure" (e-mail message to author, August 26, 2016).

17   In their autobiographies, neither Kaelter nor Plaut laments leaving Germany.

18 Damashek, *A Brand*, 54. Years later when he was looking for an explanation of how events unfolded in his life, Schaalman said, "Things happened to me that I could never have predicted nor expected."

19 Wolf, "Collected Memories," #34, 20-21.

20 Plaut, *Unfinished Business*, 34.

21 Ibid.

22 Ibid., 17.

23 Ibid., 17-18.

24 Ibid., 14.

25 Ibid.

26 Ibid., 20.

27 Ibid., 21.

28 Ibid., 23.

29 Ibid., 25.

30 Ibid., 36.

31 Ibid., 34.

32 Ibid., 39

33   Ibid. 42.

34   Ibid., 43.

35   Damashek, *A Brand*, 488.

36   Ibid., 34.

37   Ibid., 30.

38   Ibid., 40.

39   Ibid., 43.

40   Ibid., 18.

41   Ibid., 21.

42   S. Rodin-Novak, Interview with Rabbi Herman E. Schaalman, in *Chicago Jewish Historical Society* (November 26, 2001), 29.

43   Damashek, *A Brand*, 44.

44   Lee T. Bycel, *A Message to the Living: Insights and Reflections from our Rabbi, Our Teacher, and Our Friend, Rabbi Wolli Kaelter, 1914-2008*, prepared by Rabbi Lee Bycel on the occasion of Rabbi Kaelter's death (Long Beach, CA: Temple Israel, 2008), 5.

45   Gershon C. Bacon, "Virtual Jewish World: Danzig (Gdańsk), Poland," Reprinted from *Danzig 1939: Treasures of a Destroyed*

Community, Jewish Virtual Library, Retrieved May 15, 2016, from http://www.jewishvirtuallibrary.org/jsource/vjw/Danzig.html.

46 Bacon, "Virtual Jewish World: Danzig (Gdańsk), Poland."

47 Kaelter, *From Danzig*, 20.

48 Ibid., 25.

49 Ibid., 26.

50 Ibid., 34.

51 Ibid., 26.

52 This attempt to identify with cultural and religious roots is reminiscent of the strong movement that grew up in the African-American community during the 1960 and '70s. The great cultural symbol of that effort was Alex Haley's *Roots* and the TV series based on it. Not only black America, but also white America came to understand more of that heritage and the transition the former slaves had to make to a new life.

53 Kaelter, *From Danzig*, 27.

54 Ibid., 28–29.

55 Liebknecht played an important role in the development of extreme left-wing politics before and after WWI. When he was the deputy director of the Independent Social Democratic Party in Germany, he actively campaigned against the war and helped organize strikes in Germany in protest. In 1916, he was tried and convicted for

treason by a court martial. In solidarity with him, fifty-five thousand workers went on strike. See F. L. Carsten, *Revolution in Central Europe 1918–1919* (Aldershot, England: Wildwood House, 1972), 14–15.

56 Kaelter, *From Danzig*, 32. The S. A. uniform was worn by youth group members of either the Brown Shirts or the Stormtroopers.

57 Kaelter, *From Danzig*, 32.

58 Ibid.

59 Samson H. Levey, "Living history: A tribute to Rabbi Alfred Wolf," *Western States Jewish History, Vol. XXIV, No. 1,* October 1992 (Western States Jewish History Association), *77.*

60 Wolf, "Memories," #2, 1. After four years at the front, Alfred's father returned without a scratch (#31, 19). And so did Schaalman's father, who also served on the front. Plaut's father had a cushy job in the War Ministry in Berlin where he sat out the war behind a desk and was able to come home every day for lunch. It is interesting to compare this account with Schaalman's when his father returned from the front: As a two-year-old, he heard a noise in the foyer of his home and went to see what was happening. A strange man dressed in a uniform was taking off his belt and fatigue cap and hanging them in the wardrobe. Herman began to scream. "For the next several days, father and son worked at getting to know each other (Damashek, *A Brand*, 13)."

61 Ibid., #17, 11.

62 Ibid.

63   Ibid., #14, 9–10. On page 25, #41, Wolf wrote "I also considered it my duty to continue the volunteer job as a youth leader at which I had been so successful in Heidelberg. This absorbed a substantial part of my week-ends, but, of course, harmonized well with my position as a rabbinical student." He also volunteered as a youth leader when he was a rabbinic student in Berlin (#42, 25).

64   Ibid. Schaalman also expressed the same surprise that parents were willing to send their children on overnight adventures with a teenage boy. On one of these occasions, he led a small group on a skiing trip into the Alps. One night, there was such a heavy snowfall that the cabin they were staying in was nearly covered in snow. In order to get supplies, Schaalman had to exit through an attic window and construct makeshift snow shoes to get to the local village (Damashek, *A Brand*, 45).

65   Ibid., #14, 10.

66   Ibid., #21, 13.

67   Marion A. Kaplan, *Between Dignity and Despair: Jewish Life in Nazi Germany* (New York: Oxford University Press, 1998), 12.

68   W. Gunther Plaut, *The Rise of Reform Judaism* (New York: World Union for Progressive Judaism, 1963), xiv-xv. This transformation in social status was a major factor in the development of Reform Judaism.

69   Kaplan, *Between Dignity and Despair*, 74-75.

70 Kaelter, *From Danzig*, 46. Although Wolli didn't know it at the time, like Schaalman, he had a rabbinic relative in America, Samuel Rosinger, a rabbi in Beaumont, Texas. When Rosinger read in the Jewish press about the five German rabbinic students who had arrived in the United States, he contacted Kaelter and explained that he was married to a Kaelter.

71 Alfred Wolf, "Collected Memories," #37, 22–23.

72 In *Response to Modernity*, Meyer writes that their backgrounds in German Liberal Judaism were not very different from the Judaisms they encountered in America. The difference was in "emphasis" (102). Meyer's view stands in sharp contrast to the views of the rabbinic students themselves who reported that the Reform Judaism they encountered was totally foreign to them. The students thought of themselves as "crusaders on a mission to reform the heathen American Jews by teaching them what it meant to be truly Jewish" (Damashek, *A Brand*, 53ff).

73 Wolf, "Collected Memories," #35, 21.

74 There seems to be some discrepancy about the actual place. According to Wolf, the breakfast was served at the home of Dr. and Mrs. Iglauer, Glueck's in-laws ("Memories," #35, 21).

75 Damashek, *A Brand*, 59.

76 Ibid., 63.

77 Plaut, *Unfinished Business*, 54.

78 Ibid.

79 Plaut described them as communities of hope and "places of instruction and spiritual security" for people who otherwise led "constricted lives." Plaut, *Unfinished Business,* 55.

80 David Philipson Papers: Manuscript Collection No. 35 (American Jewish Archives, n. d.).

81 Kaelter, *From Danzig,* 53.

82 Plaut, *Unfinished Business,* 55.

83 Ibid., 54.

84 Folb, *An Intellectual History,* 27.

85 Rabbi Richard G. Hirsch told this writer that when he entered HUC in 1944, he "felt it was goyish: The Classical Reform services were goyish and the food service was not kosher." Damashek, *A Brand,* 519.

86 Plaut, *Unfinished Business,* 52.

87 Damashek, *A Brand,* 61.

88 Ibid.

89 Ibid., 66.

90 Ibid.

91 Plaut, *Unfinished Business*, 58.

92 Damashek, *A Brand*, 67.

93 Kaelter, *From Danzig*, 50.

94 Damashek, *A Brand*, 67.

95 Ibid.

96 Plaut, *Unfinished Business*, 59.

97 Damashek, *A Brand*, 68.

98 Ibid.

99 Ibid., 70.

100 Ibid., 74.

101 In Schaalman's thinking, God has no gender, but for the sake of stylistic simplicity and familiarity, in this text the masculine pronouns "He," "Him," "Himself" will be used. The use of the noun "God" whenever a pronominal reference is required is awkward to the English-speaking ear.

102 Later, however, reciting the prayer became customary in the dining hall. Because Morgenstern was known to have held tight rein over the college and its internal affairs, "it is fair to say that he gave his tacit consent to these new behaviors." Folb, *An Intellectual History*, 33.

103 Although Schaalman believed that Morgenstern disliked him, letters that Morgenstern had sent him from 1947–1950 are full of
expressions of warmth and care. After being presented with them
by this writer, Schaalman was deeply moved and realized that he
might have been mistaken. He remembered that, at his ordination,
Morgenstern had whispered into his ear a passage from Jeremiah
1:17–19: "Get yourself ready! Stand up and say to them whatever I
command you. Do not be terrified by them, or I will terrify you before them. Today I have made you a fortified city, an iron pillar and
a bronze wall to stand against the whole land—against the kings of
Judah, its officials, its priests and the people of the land. They will
fight against you but will not overcome you, for I am with you and
will rescue you," declares the LORD. Damashek, *A Brand,* xiii.

104 Folb, *An Intellectual History,* 25.

105 Ibid., 33. Later, however, Morgenstern criticized the rational approach to religion as inadequate and argued, "No creed can exist
entirely without ceremony."

106 Ibid.

107 E. B. Borowitz, *Studies in the Meaning of Judaism* (Philadelphia:
Jewish Publication Society, 2002), 14.

108 Richard L. Rubenstein wrote that when he was a student at HUC
in the early 1950s and had decided on a career in Jewish theology, he had to pursue his studies at a Protestant seminary: "[At
the time] there was simply no tradition of the study of contemporary theology worthy of its name in the rabbinical seminaries."
(*After Auschwitz: Radical Theology and Contemporary Judaism.*

Indianapolis: Bobbs-Merrill, 1968), 59. According to Borowitz, "The Hebrew Union College itself was unable to bring to its students a realization of theology's function and significance." He cites a 1920s HUC graduate who stated that in his day at HUC almost everyone was "for religion and against theology." (*Studies in,* 14).

109 Damashek, *A Brand,* 77.

110 Borowitz, *Studies in the Meaning of Judaism,* 49.

111 "JTS Chancellor Arnold Eisen dubbed it "the single most influential book of its generation." Zachary Silver, "The Excommunication of Mordecai Kaplan," *American Jewish Archives Journal,* 62, 1 (2010), 40, accessed September 21, 2014. http://americanjewisharchives. org/publications/journal/PDF/2010_62_01_00_silver.pdf.

112 Borowitz, *Studies in the Meaning of Judaism,* 49.

113 "Due to Kaplan's evolving position on Jewish theology, he was later condemned as a heretic by Young Israel and the rest of Orthodox Judaism, and his name is no longer mentioned in official publications as being one of the movement's founders." Jewish Virtual Library, "Rabbi Mordecai Kaplan," accessed September 23, 2008. http://www.jewishvirtuallibrary.org/jsource/biography/kaplan.html.

114 Ibid.

115 According to Schaalman, one exception to this lack of theological instruction was President Julian Morgenstern's annual address. He would use the occasion to raise fundamental theological issues. "In

general, however," Schaalman added, "because the students were typically resentful of authority, they were not receptive. In fact, they felt that the faculty treated them as if they were high school students, and they resented what they perceived as paternalism" Damashek, *A Brand*, 79.

116 Schaalman and Lichtenberg were roommates. Lichtenberg's widow remembers that their bedroom was always an obstacle course with shoes, underwear, and socks littering the floor. (Damashek, *A Brand*, 522.)

117 Damashek, *A Brand*, 81.

118 Avraham Barkai, "Jewish Life under Persecution," ed. M. A. Meyer and M. Brenner, *German Jewish History in Modern Times: Renewal and Destruction 1918–1945* (New York: Columbia University Press, 1998), 231–257.

119 Ibid.

120 Ibid.

121 Damashek, *A Brand*, 86.

122 Ibid., 87.

123 Wolf, "Memories," #30, 19.

124 Abraham J. Peck, *The German-Jewish Legacy in America: 1938–1988* (Detroit: Wayne State University Press, 1990), 6. According

to Peck, the German-Jewish exodus from Germany to America "peaked" after *Kristallnacht*.

125 Later, Freddie made *Aliyah* to Israel and settled in Mea Shearim, the Orthodox neighborhood in Jerusalem. Freddie had chosen to be an Orthodox Jew and led a life very different from his bother Herman. By 2015, when I visited Freddie in Jerusalem, his family had grown to twenty-eight, including grandchildren and two Orthodox rabbis.

126 Wolf, "Memories," #53, 32. At first the synagogue was spared, but after higher authorities threatened to send in outside SS troopers if the locals didn't burn it down, someone torched the building. The Jewish community, however, managed to save the Torah scrolls.

127 Helmut Joho, *Eberbacher Geschichts Blatt* (Eberbach, Germany: Druckerei and Verlag Wilhel Krauth, 1989), 46.

128 Ibid.

129 Ibid. Franz's imprisonment was only the beginning of the Kaelter family's ordeal. Several family members died in the Holocaust, including Wolli's paternal aunt, Flore, her husband, and two aunts on his father's side, Bianca and Hede.

130 George Fogelson, "Interview with Rabbi Wolli Kaelter," JewishGen Danzig/Gdańsk SIG, accessed September 29, 2015, http://www.jewishgen.org/Danzig/wkaelter.php.

131 Abraham J. Peck, *The German-Jewish Legacy in America: 1938–1988* (Detroit: Wayne State University Press, 1989), 6.

132 According to Dan Wolf, "When Dad proposed, Mom said no, because it was the Depression and she was sure her family (her mother, aunt, two sisters and a brother) couldn't survive without the $15/week she made at National Cash Register. When her mother found out, she told Mom to go back and tell him Yes!" (Dan Wolf, e-mail message to author, August 26, 2016).

133 Hilda Lichtenberg, Interview, 13.

134 Plaut, *Unfinished Business*, 84. Plaut served in that post until 1948.

135 According to Joseph Topek, Lichtenberg was one of the Hillel rabbis who went to war as a chaplain. "Hillel Rabbis off to War," *Hillel: The Foundation of Campus Life*, accessed July 8, 2013, http://www.hillel.org/about/facts/rabbis_and_war_2008.htm. HUC contributed to the war effort by accelerating its rabbinic studies program to prepare students to take over for rabbis who went into the service, and Jewish leaders had been asking their member congregations to give their rabbis leaves of absence for the duration of the war. By the end of 1943, the army had fifty-eight Jewish chaplains on active duty, and the navy had six. *American Jewish Year Book*, 1942–1943, 97.

136 Karl Richter, "A Refugee Rabbinate," in *The Jewish Legacy and the German Conscience: Essays in Memory of Rabbi Joseph Asher*, edited by Moses Rischin and Rapheal Asher (Berkeley, CA: The Judah L. Magnes Museum, 1991), 209.

137 Ibid.

138 Damashek, *A Brand*, 386.

139 C. A. Kroloff, "Unity within Diversity." In J. B. Glaser (ed.), *Tanu Rabbanan: Our Rabbis Taught: Essays on the Occasion of the Centennial of the Central Conference of American Rabbis, 1989 Yearbook, II,* (New York: Central Conference of American Rabbis, 1990), 189-103.

140 "Reform Judaism: The Columbus Platform 1937," *The Jewish Virtual Library,* accessed September 17, 2015, https://www.jewishvirtuallibrary.org/jsource/Judaism/Columbus_platform.html.

141 For an excellent account of the history of Reform's movement toward traditional practice and observance, see Meyer's *Response to Modernity*, 322–325. Two more recent books bring that history into the twenty-first century, Michael Meyer and David Meyers, ed., *Between Jewish Tradition and Modernity* (Detroit: Wayne State University Press, 2014), and W. Gunther Plaut's *The Growth of Reform Judaism: American and European Sources* (New York: The Jewish Publication Society, 2015). The publication is a revised edition of his 1963 *The Rise of Reform Judaism*. See particularly Howard A. Berman's "Introduction," and David Ellenson's "Epilogue—Reform Judaism After 1948.

142 Dan Wolf provided this information regarding his father's theological views: "Dad's grandfather, Benjamin, raised him very traditionally, but Dad very consciously chose the German Liberal movement. I strongly suspect that, after the initial shock of some of the Reform practices, he became comfortable with this more

modern and critically-open approach to Judaism" (Dan Wolf, e-mail message to author, August 26, 2016).

143 Michael Meyer, "The Refugee Scholars Project of the Hebrew Union College," in *Jacob Rader Marcus: An Appreciation*, edited by Alfred Gottschalk (Waltham, MA; New York: KTAV, 1976), 359–75. See also Richter, "A Refugee Rabbinate," 210.

144 Ibid. Although not specifically addressing the contribution of the Gang of Five, Michael Meyer claims that the refugee rabbis who left Germany in what is known as the "fourth wave of immigration" made a large contribution to Jewish life in the countries where they ultimately settled. In America, they were "among the most prominent leaders of American Reform Judaism," as were their more traditional colleagues, "who had at least studied in Germany," and helped to shape Conservative and Orthodox Judaism.

145 Damashek, *A Brand*, 383.

146 Jacob Sarna, "The Crucial Decade in Jewish Camping" in *A Place of Their Own: The Rise of Reform Jewish Camping* (Tuscaloosa: University of Alabama Press, 2006), 36.

147 Ibid.

148 Lorge and Zola, 54.

149 UAHC, 64.

150 Sarna, "The Crucial Decade," 28.

151 Damashek, *A Brand*, 213. Schaalman considerd his contribution to establishing a summer camp for Jewish children the most important achievement of his long and distinguished career. Rabbi Richard G. Hirsch offers a similar assessment: "The most important thing he did was establish the camp, which, along with the establishment of the Religious Action Center, had more impact on Reform Judaism than anything else in the last half of the twentieth century." Richard G. Hirsch, "Interview with Richard Damashek [Digital Recording]," (Cincinnati: American Jewish Archives, March 26, 2010).

152 Sarna, "The Crucial Decade," 28.

153 Dan Wolf, e-mail message to author, August 26, 2016.

154 Sarna, 45.

155 Ibid., 37.

156 Meyer, *Response to Modernity*, 354.

157 Meyer, *Response to Modernity*, 362. See also W. G. Plaut and M. A. Meyer, *The Reform Jewish Reader* (New York: UAHC Press, 2001), 41. The first conference in 1956 attracted thirty-five rabbis including Reform Rabbis Eugene Borowitz, Jakob Petuchowski, David Polish, Steven Schwarzschild, Bernard Martin, Arnold Wolf, Emil Fackenheim, and W. Gunther Plaut. Orthodox Judaism was represented by Rabbis Zalman Schacter-Shalomi, Irving (Yitz) Greenberg, and David Hartman.

158 Plaut and Schaalman were the only two of The Gang who attended these meetings. There are no indications in Wolf's "Memoirs"
or Kaelter's *From Danzig* that they were experiencing theological
challenges, nor is there any document indicating that Lichtenberg
shared them.

159 Damashek, *A Brand*, 370.

160 P. Ochs, "The Emergence of Postmodern Jewish Theology and
Philosophy," in P. Ochs (ed.) *Reviewing the Covenant* (Albany: State
University of New York Press, 2000), 5, 14.

161 Damashek, *A Brand*, 376. The growing awareness of the Holocaust
was beginning to raise questions about the existence of God and
God's nature. Lurking in the background for Jews and Jewish theologians was the question: where was God during the Holocaust?
That unease took another fifteen years to break out into theological discussion and gave birth to the "Death of God" movement.
Surprisingly, the movement had a stronger impact on Christian
theologians than it did on the rabbinic community across all denom-
inations. In his *After Auschwitz: Radical Theology and Contemporary
Judaism* (1966), Richard Rubenstein raised considerable controversy
among his rabbinic colleagues, although not at first.

162 W. G. Plaut, *The Growth of Reform Judaism* (New York: World
Union for Progressive Judaism, 1965), 351.

163 3Ibid.

164 Plaut, *More Unfinished Business*, 110.

165 This battle shaped the direction of Reform for the next four decades, but for those who wanted more autonomy, it was a losing
battle. By 1998, Reform restated its principles in a new "Statement
of Principles for Reform Judaism." On one hand, it was an attempt
to provide continuity with the original "1885 Pittsburgh Platform,"
and on the other, to point forward to a more spiritual and tradition-
based Judaism.

166 D. E. Kaplan, *American Reform Judaism: An Introduction* (New
Brunswick, NJ: Rutgers University Press, 2003), 64.

167 Plaut, *More Unfinished Business*, 111–112.

168 I. H. Fishbein, "Central Conference of American Rabbis: Report
of Committee on Mixed Marriage: Minority Report" (Rabbinic
Center for Research and Counseling, June 19, 1973), accessed June
19, 2008, http://www.rcrconline.org/resourc2.htm.

169 Cf. Damashek, *A Brand*, 266–267. Another issue confronting
the CCAR leadership was that its rabbis who refused to perform
interfaith marriages were having trouble getting jobs in congregations that used as a hiring criterion the candidate's willingness to perform interfaith marriages. Established rabbis also were
feeling pressure from their congregants and their boards. Some
found ways to salve their consciences by imposing conditions
that the couple agree to keep a Jewish home and raise their children as Jews.

170 Herman E. Schaalman, "Paper" (CCAR Archives, 1, Feb. 10, 1971).

171 Folb, *An Intellectual History*, 57.

172 Damashek, *A Brand*, 269.

173 J. D. Sarna and J. Golden, "The American Jewish Experience in the Twentieth Century: Antisemitism and Assimilation" (National Humanities Center.org, October 2000), accessed June 20, 2008, from http:// nationalhumanitiescenter.org/tserve/twenty/tkeyinfo/ jewishexpb.htm.4

174 Cf. E. J. Lipman, *Tanu Rabbanan: Our Masters Have Taught Us*, in *Tanu Rabbanan: Our Rabbis Taught: Essays on the Occasion of the Centennial of the Central Conference of American Rabbis, 1989 Yearbook, II*, ed. J. B. Glaser (New York: Central Conference of American Rabbis, 1990), 39–70; and "World Jewish Population 2012" (University of Connecticut: Berman Institute—North American Jewish Data Bank, Number 7—2012), accessed December 1, 2015, http://www. jewishdatabank.org/studies/downloadFile.cfm?FileID=2941.

175 Ibid.

176 Plaut, *More Unfinished Business*, 114–115.

177 D. Marmur, "American Reform: Observations from the Margin," in D. E. Kaplan (ed.) *Platforms and Prayer Books* (New York: Rowman & Littlefield Publishers, Inc., 2002), 287.

178 Central Conference of American Rabbis (CCAR), "Report of the Committee on Patrilineal Descent on the Status of Children of Mixed Marriages," CCAR Yearbook, (93): Columbus, OH, 1983, 159–160.

179 Plaut, *More Unfinished Business*, 129–130.

180 Ibid., 144. Even that decision was controversial. Among the Israeli rabbis, some refused to recognize as legitimate the Orthodox credentials of some of their rabbinic colleagues. These divisions in the Israeli rabbinate created a nightmare for Jews by choice.

181 Folb, *An Intellectual History*, 78.

182 Richard G. Hirsch, "Interview with Richard Damashek" (Cincinnati: American Jewish Archives, March 26, 2010).

183 As late as 2016 at the age of one hundred, he has continued to speak out against Reform's current direction.

184 According to E. B. Borowitz, the time was not yet ripe for such an undertaking [*Studies in the Meaning of Judaism* (Philadelphia: Jewish Publication Society, 2002), 14]. Not until the beginning of the twenty-first century did Reform Judaism undergo a significant change from the days when its "rabbis rejected theology almost completely." A defining point in this transformation came in 1999, when, after years of study, the CCAR issued a new platform that would recapture old and provide new pathways to holiness and social justice. The new "Statement of Principles for Reform Judaism" was an attempt to provide continuity with the original "1885 Pittsburgh Platform" and to point forward to a more spiritual and tradition-based Judaism. [P. J. Haas, "Reform and Halacha: A Rapprochement?" in D. E. Kaplan (ed.) *Platform and Prayer Books*, (Lanham, MD: Rowman & Littlefield Publishers, 2002) 233–246].

185 Ruth Levor, Hebrew Union College Memorial Talk (unpublished manuscript), January 2015.

186 B'nai B'rith Hillel Commission and B'nai B'rith Hillel Directors, Leo Lichtenberg (unpublished biography), August 3, 1977.

187 Ibid.

188 For a discussion of the politics of intermarriage within the Reform Movement during the twentieth century, cf. Richard Damashek, *A Brand*, 266–272.

189 Ibid.

190 Kaelter, *From Danzig*, xv.

191 Samson H. Levey, "Living History: A Tribute to Rabbi Alfred Wolf," *Western States Jewish History*, Vol. XXIV, No. 1, October 1992 (Western States Jewish History Association), 77.

192 Schaalman, too, devoted his life to interfaith communication because he believed that lack of understanding was the cause of Germany's rejection of its Jews.

193 Wolf, "Collected Memories," #243, 123. As we will see, this kind of friendship between a rabbi and a priest was not unique to Wolf. In the late 1980s, Schaalman developed such a close friendship with Chicago's Archbishop Bernardin that, as he was dying, Bernardin asked him to participate in his funeral.

194 AJA Biographical Sketch. Gunther Plaut Papers. Manuscript Collection No. 743 1934–1994, accessed December 30, 2014, http://americanjewisharchives.org/collections/ms0743/#bio.

195 Ron Csillag, "Scholar Urged Jews to Engage Larger World," accessed June 21, 2016, http://v1.theglobeandmail.com/servlet/story/LAC.20120214.OBPLAUT0214ATL/BDAStory/BDA/deaths/?pageRequested=all.

196 Plaut, *Unfinished Business*, 213.

197 A comprehensive guide for Reform Judaism for observance throughout the life cycle. It includes sections on everything from birth, naming and covenantal rituals, adoption, childhood, marriage, divorce, to ethical wills and death.

198 In his introduction to the *Manual*, Plaut took the position that God required that Shabbat observance was a *mitzvah* and therefore a requirement for Jews. This position got him into trouble with his colleagues.

199 Plaut, *More Unfinished Business*, 151.

200 David E. S. Stein, New York: [Union for Reform Judaism] URJ, 2006, 1604 pp. Reviewed by David J. Zucker.

201 Margalit Fox, "W. Gunther Plaut Dies at 99," 28.

202 Jonathan V. Plaut, forward to *Through the Sound of Many Voices: Writings Contributed on the Occasion of the 70th Birthday of W.*

Gunther Plaut, ed. Jonathan V. Plaut (Toronto: Lester & Orpen Dennys Publisher, 1982), x–xi.

203 Richter, "A Refugee Rabbinate," 215.

204 R. R. Weiman, "Putting the Fragments Together. Ten Minutes of Torah," (Union of Reform Judaism, February 7, 2006), accessed December 28, 2008, http://tmt.urj.net/archives/2socialaction/020706. htm.

BIBLIOGRAPHY

Alexander, Robert J. *International Trotskyism, 1929–1985: A Documented Analysis of the Movement.* Durham, NC: Duke University Press, 1991.

Bacon, Gershon C. "Virtual Jewish World: Danzig (Gdańsk), Poland," Reprinted from *Danzig 1939: Treasures of a Destroyed Community*, Jewish Virtual Library, accessed May 15, 2016, http://www.jewish-virtuallibrary.org/jsource/vjw/Danzig.html.

Barkai, A. "Jewish Life under Persecution. In *German-Jewish History in Modern Times: Renewal and Destruction 1918–1945*, edited by M. A. Meyer and M. Brenner (New York: Columbia University Press, 1998) 231-257.

———. "Population Decline and Economic Stagnation." In *German-Jewish History in Modern Times: Renewal and Destruction 1918–1945*, edited by M. A. Meyer and M. Brenner (New York: Columbia University Press, 1998), 30-44.

Berman, Howard A., Introduction to W. Gunther Plaut's *The Growth of Reform Judaism: American and European Sources*, New York: The

Jewish Publication Society, 2015, xxxiii-xliv. The publication is a revised edition of Plaut's *The Rise of Reform Judaism* (1963).

Borowitz, E. B. *Studies in the Meaning of Judaism* Philadelphia: Jewish Publication Society, 2002.

Bycel, Lee T. *A Message to the Living: Insights and Reflections from our Rabbi, Our Teacher, and Our Friend, Rabbi Wolli Kaelter, 1914–2008*, prepared by Rabbi Lee Bycel on the occasion of Rabbi Kaelter's death. Long Beach, CA: Temple Israel, 2008.

Carsten, F. L. *Revolution in Central Europe 1918–1919*. Aldershot, England: Wildwood House, 1972.

Damashek, Richard. *A Brand Plucked from the Fire: The Life of Rabbi Herman E. Schaalman*. Jersey City, NJ: KTAV Publishing House, Inc., 2013.

Ellenson, David, "Epilogue to the 50th Anniversary Edition," in W. Gunther Plaut's *The Growth of Reform Judaism: American and European Sources*. New York: The Jewish Publication Society, 2015, 363-384.

Fishbein, I. H. "Central Conference of American Rabbis: Report of Committee on Mixed Marriage: Minority Report." Rabbinic Center for Research and Counseling, June 19, 1973, accessed June 19, 2008, http://www.rcrconline.org/resourc2.htm.

Fogelson, George. "Interview with Rabbi Wolli Kaelter," JewishGen Danzig/Gdańsk SIG, accessed September 29, 2015, http://www.jewishgen.org/Danzig/wkaelter.php.

Fox, Margalit. "W. Gunther Plaut, Defined Reform Judaism, Dies at 99." *New York Times*, February 11, 2012, accessed December 30, 2014, http://www.nytimes.com/2012/02/12/world/americas/w-gunther-plaut-rabbi-and-scholar-dies-at-99.html?pagewanted=all&_r=0, 28.

Goldring/Woldenberg Institute of Southern Jewish Life. "Encyclopedia of Southern Jewish Communities—Wichita Falls, Texas," accessed August 4, 2014, http://www.isjl.org/texas-wichita-falls-encyclopedia.html.

Hirsch, Richard G. "Interview with Richard Damashek [Digital Recording]." Cincinnati: American Jewish Archives, March 26, 2010.

Joho, Helmut. *Eberbacher Geschichts Blatt.* Eberbach, Germany: Druckerei and Verlag Wilhel Krauth, 1989.

Jewish Virtual Library. "Rabbi Mordecai Kaplan," accessed September 23, 2008, http://www.jewishvirtuallibrary.org/jsource/biography/kaplan.html.

The Jewish Virtual Library. "Reform Judaism: The Columbus Platform 1937," accessed September 17, 2015, https://www.jewishvirtuallibrary.org/jsource/Judaism/Columbus_platform.html.

Kaelter, Wolli, and G. Cohn. *From Danzig: An American Rabbi's Journey.* Malibu, CA: Pangloss Press, 1997.

Kaplan, D. E. *American Reform Judaism: An Introduction.* New Brunswick, NJ: Rutgers University Press, 2003.

Kaplan, Marion A. *Between Dignity and Despair: Jewish Life in Nazi Germany.* New York: Oxford University Press, 1998.

Kroloff, C. A. "Unity within Diversity." In *Tanu Rabbanan: Our Rabbis Taught: Essays on the Occasion of the Centennial of the Central Conference of American Rabbis, 1989 Yearbook, II*, edited by J. B. Glaser (New York: Central Conference of American Rabbis, 1990), 89-103.

Levor, Ruth. E-mail message to author, June 31, 2015.

Lichtenberg, Gershom. E-mail to Richard Damashek, June 30, 2015.

Lichtenberg, Hilda. Interview by Barbara Kreisis. American Jewish Archives, Jan. 15, 1981.

Lipman, E. J. *Tanu Rabbanan: Our Masters Have Taught Us*. In *Tanu Rabbanan: Our Rabbis Taught: Essays on the Occasion of the Centennial of the Central Conference of American Rabbis, 1989 Yearbook, II*, edited by J. B. Glaser. New York: Central Conference of American Rabbis, 1990; and "World Jewish Population 2012" University of Connecticut: Berman Institute—North American Jewish Data Bank, Number 7—2012, accessed December 1, 2015, http://www.jewishdatabank.org/studies/downloadFile.cfm?File ID=2941.

Lorge, Michael M. and Gary P. Zola. "The Beginnings of Union Institute in Oconomowoc, Wisconsin." In *A Place of Our Own*, edited by Michael M. Lorge and Gary P. Zola, 52-84. Tuscaloosa: The University of Alabama Press, 2006.

Marmur, D. "American Reform: Observations from the Margin," in D. E. Kaplan (ed.) *Platforms and Prayer Books*. New York: Rowman & Littlefield Publishers, Inc., 2002.

Meyer, Michael A. *Response to Modernity.* New York: Oxford University Press, 1988.

————. "The Refugee Scholars Project of the Hebrew Union College," in *Jacob Rader Marcus: An Appreciation*, edited by Alfred Gottschalk (Waltham, MA; New York: KTAV, 1976), 359-375.

Meyer, Michael. A., and David N. Meyers, (ed.), *Between Jewish Tradition and Modernity.* Detroit: Wayne State University Press, 2014.

Ochs, Peter. "The Emergence of Postmodern Jewish Theology and Philosophy." In *Reviewing the Covenant*, edited by Peter Ochs. (Albany: State University of New York Press, 2000), 3-34.

Peck, Abraham J. *The German-Jewish Legacy in America: 1938–1988.* Detroit: Wayne State University Press, 1990.

Philipson, David. Papers: Manuscript Collection No. 35. Cincinnati: American Jewish Archives, n. d.

Plaut, W. Gunther and M. A. Meyer. *The Reform Jewish Reader.* New York: UAHC Press, 2001.

Plaut, W. Gunther. *The Rise of Reform Judaism.* New York: World Union for Progressive Judaism, 1963.

————. *Unfinished Business: An Autobiography.* Toronto: Lester & Orpen Dennys, Ltd., 1981.

————. *More Unfinished Business.* Toronto: University of Toronto Press, 1997.

Richter, Karl L. "A Refugee Rabbinate," in *The Jewish Legacy and the German Conscience: Essays in Memory of Rabbi Joseph Asher*, edited by Moses Rischin and Rapheal Asher (Berkeley, CA: The Judah L. Magnes Museum, 1991), 205-218.

Rodin-Novak, S. Interview with Rabbi Herman E. Schaalman, in *Chicago Jewish Historical Society*. November 26, 2001.

Rubenstein, Richard L. *After Auschwitz: Radical Theology and Contemporary Judaism*. Indianapolis: Bobbs-Merrill, 1968.

Sarna, Jacob. "The Crucial Decade in Jewish Camping" in *A Place of Their Own: The Rise of Reform Jewish Camping*, edited by Michael M. Lorge and Gary P. Zola, 27-51. Tuscaloosa: University of Alabama Press, 2006.

Sarna, J. D., and J. Golden. "The American Jewish Experience in the Twentieth Century: Antisemitism and Assimilation." National Humanities Center.org, October 2000, accessed June 20, 2008, from http://nationalhumanitiescenter.org/tserve/twenty/tkeyinfo/jewishexpb.htm.

Schaalman, Herman E. interview [Richard Damashek, interviewer], March 16, 2014.

———. Interview with Richard Damashek [digital recording], *American Jewish Archives*, May 16, 2013.

———. Interview with Richard Damashek [digital recording], *American Jewish Archives*, November 20, 2006.

———. "Paper." CCAR Archives, 1, Feb. 10, 1971.

Silver, Zackary. "The Excommunication of Mordecai Kaplan," *American Jewish Archives Journal*, 62, 1 (2010), 40, accessed September 21, 2014, http://americanjewisharchives.org/publications/journal/ PDF/2010_62_01_00_silver.pdf.

Topek, Joseph. "Hillel Rabbis off to War," *Hillel: The Foundation of Campus Life. American Jewish Year Book*, 1942–1943, accessed July 8, 2013, http://www.hillel.org/about/facts/rabbis_and_war_2008. htm.

UAHC, 77–80th Annual Report, 64.

Wolf, A. "Collected Memories of Rabbi Alfred Wolf, aka Dad, aka Papa." Unpublished manuscript, 1986.

ABOUT THE AUTHOR

––––––

RICHARD DAMASHEK, PHD, SPENT HIS career as a college English professor. He received his bachelor's degree in English and comparative literature from Rutgers University, his master's degree at Columbia University, and his doctorate at the University of Wisconsin.

In 2013, Damashek published *A Brand Plucked from the Fire*, his biography of Rabbi Herman E. Schaalman. His latest book, *The Gang of Five*, expands the scope of his research to examine the lives of five German refugee rabbinic students from their early lives in Germany to their remarkable impact on twentieth-century Reform Judaism. Damashek recently contributed his essay, "Questioning God's Omnipotence and Omniscience: The Evidence in Torah," to the anthology *A Life of Meaning: The Essential Guide to Reform Judaism*. His next writing project will be an unorthodox approach to the study of the Books of Genesis and Exodus.

When he's not busy researching and writing, Damashek loves spending time with his wife, Jane, and traveling to distant lands. Whenever possible, he enjoys spending time with his children and grandchildren. He and his wife live a happy life in retirement in St. Petersburg, Florida.

INDEX

Britain *17*
Brittanic *55*
Buber, Martin *20, 30, 38*
Buddhist *106*
B'nai B'rith Hillel Commission *135*

C

Camp Hess Kramer *91-92, 106*
Camp Saratoga (later renamed "Camp Swig") *91*
Canada *xxii, 33, 109*
Canadian Jewish Congress *108*
Casablanca *80*
Catholic *44, 106, 108*
Central Conference of American Rabbis (CCAR) *59, 88, 92, 98, 95, 97-104, 107-109, 111, 169n133, 184n135*
Charlottesville, Virginia *103*
Chicago *85, 107-108, 193n136*
Christian (s) *47, 106, 161n132*
Cincinnati, Ohio *xx, xxv, xxix, 1, 4, 49, 56-58, 60, 64, 66-67, 74, 79, 81-84*
Civilization: Toward a Reconstruction of American Jewish Life (1934), Mordecai Kaplan 72

Classical Reform Judaism *58-59, 63, 87-88, 92, 94, 85n122*
Cohen, Alfred *79*
Cohen, Rabbi Morton *58-59*
Cohen, Sally *58, 60*
Cologne Synagogue *86*
Columbus Platform (1937) *88*
Commentary 109
Committee on Mixed Marriage *xxii, 75, 95, 100-102, 107*
Committee on Patrilineal Descent *xxii, 95, 99-102, 107*
Communist Party *14, 38-39*
Confessionslos 27
Conservative Judaism *xxvi, 24, 102, 145n130*
Council of Religious Leaders of Metropolitan Chicago *107*
Covenantal Theologians *94-97*
Covenantal Theology *94-97*
Csillag, Ron *108*
Cuba *85*

D

Dachau *78-80*
Danzig (Gedansk), Poland *32-35, 40, 80-81, 56n118, 70n120, 158n131*
Dayton, Ohio *83*

Rabbinic officiation at interfaith (mixed) marriages *97-
102*
Ranshoff, Nathan *57, 80*
Rathenau, Walter *10*
Reden über das Judentum (Martin Buber, 1923) *38*
Reform Jewish Camping (see
also "Gindling Hilltop
Camp," "Camp Hess Kram-
er," "Olin Sang Ruby Union
Institute," and "Camp Saratoga (Swig)" *xxii, xxvi, 90-
92, 151n130*
Reform Judaism (Reform movement *xvii, xix, xxvi-xxvii, xxix,
1, 5-6, 22, 37, 41, 52, 60-62, 67,
71-72, 87-112, 68n120, 72n121,
125n126, 141n129, 144n130,
151n130, 151n130, 165n132,
184n135, 188n135, 197n136*
Regensburg, Germany *30*
Reichsbanner (a militia sponsored by the Social Demo-
cratic and the Democratic
Parties) *46*
Reichstag *46*
Reinhardt, Max *13*
Return to Germany *20, 75-77*
Revelation at Sinai (see Covenantal Theology and Cov-
enantal Theologians) *95*

Richter, Karl *87, 91, 103, 111*
Rilke, Rainer Maria *13*
Ritter von Epp, Franz *26*
Rockdale Temple *38-39, 60*
Rosenberg, Bernie *65*
Rosenzweig, Franz *38*
Rostock, Germany *49*
Rubenstein, Richard *161n132*
Russian Jews *33*

S

SA *27, 39, 44, 76,*
Sarna, Jacob *90, 173n133*
Saxony, Germany *34*
Schaalman, Adolf (Rabbi
Schaalman's father) *22-23,
30, 75, 78-79*
Schaalman, Ernst (Rabbi Schaalman's brother) *22, 78-79*
Schaalman, Lotte (nee Stern,
Rabbi Schaalman's wife) *75,
91*
Schaalman, Manfred ("Freddie," Rabbi Schaalman's
brother) *22, 78-79, 125n126*
Schaalman, Rabbi Herman E.
*xxii, xxv-xxvi, xxix, 2-6, 36-
38, 44, 49, 51, 55-58, 60-75,
77-79, 85, 87, 89-100, 102-
103, 108-109, 111, 1n113,
17n115, 119n115. 64n120,*

West Coast *12, 14, 61, 68-69*
West Prussia *32*
Wichita Falls, Texas *58, 67, 86*
Wilshire Boulevard Temple *61-62, 69*
Wolf, Arnold *157n131*
Wolf, Herman (Rabbi Alfred Wolf's father) *36, 37, 56, 75*
Wolf, Martin *23*
Wolf, Rabbi Alfred *xxii, xxv-xxvi, xxix, 2-5, 21, 41-49, 52, 54, 56-58, 105-106, 111, 13n115, 60n119, Herman (Alfred's father) 36, 37, 56, 75, Regine (Alfred's mother) 41, Benjamin Levy (Alfred's grandfather) 44-45, 80, Camp Gindling Hilltop 106, Camp Hess Kramer 91, 96, Camp Saratoga (Swig) 91, Eberbach, Germany 41-48, 76, 79, 80, Fleitz 48, 76, 79-80, Frohmann 45, Hitler 43-44, HUC 61-85, Kristallnacht 78-80, Lehranstalt xx, xxix, 1, 4, 18, 31, 48-49, 2n113, 4n114, Marriage 83, 91-92, Nazis 44-48, Ordination 2, 22, 32, 60, 63, 69, 83-85, 99, 103n123, Our American Heritage 109, Pinkuss, Dr. 45, Rabbi Magnin 106, Skirball Institute 107, UAHC 91, West Coast director UAHC 91, 106, Wilshire Boulevard Temple 61-62, 69,*
World Union of Progressive Judaism *102*
World War I *7, 15, 32, 41, 55n118*
World War II *90*

Y

Youth-groups *30, 36*

Z

Zionism (Zionists) *9-10, 20-21, 30, 37, 69, 71, 90*
Zola, Gary *xxvi, 4n113*
Zoppot, a village in Germany *80*
Zucker, David J. *109*
Zweig, Arnold *13*

Made in the USA
Lexington, KY
21 May 2017